THE WALL STREET JOURNAL
ON
MANAGEMENT

THE WALL STREET JOURNAL
ON
MANAGEMENT

The Best of the
Manager's Journal

Edited by

David Asman and Adam Meyerson

DOW JONES-IRWIN
Homewood, Illinois 60430

ISBN 0-87094-685-4
Library of Congress Catalog Card No.
85–71919

Printed in the United States of America

1 2 3 4 5 6 7 8 9 0 K 2 1 0 9 8 7 6 5

Introduction

The idea for this book comes from readers of *The Wall Street Journal.* Enthusiasm for the weekly Manager's Journal column has grown steadily since its inception in 1979. Copies of articles have often been posted on company bulletin boards, distributed at board meetings, and taught in business school curricula. As editors of the column (Meyerson was editor until 1983, Asman afterward), we received an increasing number of suggestions to put together a book of the best of the Manager's Journal.

Our goals in editing the Manager's Journal column were always simple. We sought practical advice about the real-life dilemmas that every manager must grapple with. We sought the same kind of lively, jargon-free writing that the rest of *The Wall Street Journal* is known for. And we focused on management problems that were narrow enough to be covered sufficiently in a short space, but broad enough to be of interest to general readers.

One of our great joys as editors was to discover how well managers and consultants can write when they tell stories and draw down-to-earth generalizations based on their own business experiences. Too often business writing is colorless and preachy. But managers can be just as entertaining and informative in their writing as they are in their conversations with friends and business associates. And when they focus on the subjects that they know best, managers have an incredible amount of wisdom to share. The Manager's Journal column, and this book, try to capture some of this wisdom, and to make it accessible to the broadest possible audience.

David Asman and Adam Meyerson

Contents

1

Making the Most of Yourself

2

Technology

3

People You Work With

4

Strategy

5

Hiring and Firing

6

Protecting Your Company

7

Family and Friends

1

Making the Most of Yourself

Your Most Precious Resource: Your Time

By Andrew S. Grove

A great deal of a manager's work has to do with allocating resources: manpower, money and capital. But the single most important resource that we allocate from one moment to the next is our own time. How you handle your own time is, in my view, the single most important aspect of being a role model and leader.

A manager must keep many balls in the air at the same time and shift his energy and attention to activities that will most increase the output of his organization. In other words, he should move to the point where his *leverage* will be the greatest.

Much of my day is spent acquiring information. I read standard reports and memos but also get information ad hoc. I talk to people inside and outside the company, managers at other firms, financial analysts and members of the press. Customer complaints are, for instance, a very important source of information. This includes internal customers as well. The Intel training organization, which I serve as an instructor, is an internal customer of mine. To cut myself off from the casual complaints of people in that group would be a mistake because I would miss getting an evaluation of my performance as an internal "supplier."

I have to confess that the type of information most useful

to me, and I suspect most useful to all managers, comes from quick, often casual conversational exchanges, many of them on the telephone. These usually reach a manager much faster than anything written down. And usually the more timely the information, the more valuable it is.

So why are written reports necessary at all? They obviously can't provide timely information. What they do is constitute an archive of data, help to validate ad hoc inputs and catch, in safety-net fashion, anything you may have missed. But reports also have another, totally different function. As they are formulated and written, the author is forced to be more precise than he might be orally. Hence their value stems from the discipline and the thinking the writer is forced to impose upon himself as he identifies and deals with trouble spots. Reports are more a *medium* of *self-discipline* than a way to convey information. *Writing* the report is important; reading it often is not.

There is an especially efficient way to get information, much neglected by most managers. That is to visit a particular place in the company and observe what's going on there. Think of what happens when somebody comes to see a manager in his office. A certain stop-and-start dynamic occurs when the visitor sits down, something socially dictated. While a two-minute kernel of information is exchanged, the meeting often takes a half-hour. But if a manager walks through an area and sees a person with whom he has a two-minute concern, he can simply stop, cover his subject and be on his way.

It's obvious that the quality of your decision-making depends on how well you comprehend the facts and issues in your business. This is why information-gathering is so important in a manager's life. Other activities—conveying information, making decisions and being a role model for your subordinates—are also governed by the *base of information* that you have. In short, information-gathering is the basis of all other managerial work, which is why I choose to spend so much of my day doing it.

You often do things at the office designed to influence events slightly, maybe making a phone call to an associate suggesting that a decision be made in a certain way, or sending a note or a memo that shows how you see a particular situation, or making a comment during an oral presentation. In such instances you may be advocating a preferred course of action, but you are not issuing an instruction or a command. Yet you're doing something stronger than merely conveying information. Let's call it "nudging" because through it you nudge an individual or a meeting in the direction you would like. This is an immensely important managerial activity in which we engage all the time, and it should be carefully distinguished from decision-making that results in firm, clear directives. For every decision we make, we probably nudge things a dozen times.

Finally, there is a subtle aspect of our work that we all must consider. While we move about, doing what we regard as our jobs, we are role models for people in our organization—our subordinates, our peers and even our supervisors. Much has been said and written about a manager's need to be a leader. The fact is, no single managerial activity can be said to constitute leadership, and nothing leads as well as example. Values and behavioral norms are simply not transmitted easily by talk or memo, but are conveyed very effectively by doing and doing visibly.

Don't think for a moment that the way I've described leadership applies only to large operations. An insurance agent in a small office who continually talks with personal friends on the phone imparts a set of values about permissible conduct to everyone working for him. A lawyer who returns to his office after lunch a little drunk does the same. On the other hand, a supervisor in a company, large or small, who takes his work seriously exemplifies to his associates the most important managerial value of all.

On a typical working day, I participate in some 25 separate activities, mostly information-gathering and information-giving, but also decision-making and nudging. I spend two-thirds of my time in a meeting of one kind or another. Before you are horrified at how much time I spend in meetings answer one question: Which of the activities—information-gathering, information-giving, decision-making, nudging and being a role model—could I have performed outside a meeting? The answer is practically none.

When I look at my schedule, I don't see any obvious patterns. I deal with things in seemingly random fashion, and my day always ends when I'm tired, not when I am done. A manager's work is never done: There is always more to be done, more that should be done, always more that can be done. That is why choosing and performing activities with high leverage is the key to managerial effectiveness.

Mr. Grove is president of Intel Corp. His article is excerpted and adapted from his book, "High Output Management," published by Random House.

Building Endurance

By Mortimer R. Feinberg
and Aaron Levenstein

Helen Hayes once made a shrewd observation that is as pertinent to business leadership as it is to her own profession of acting. Talent and ability are not enough, she said. "Nothing is any good without endurance."

We've all known intelligent and capable executives who have failed because they didn't have enough emotional and physical stamina. Ecclesiastes noted that the race is not necessarily to the swift. The challenge is to keep running. So, too, in business, what often counts is the ability to work consistently long and hard, especially under pressure and after disappointing setbacks.

Fatigue leads to a loss of efficiency, impaired initiative, distorted judgment, skewed perception of time and heightened anxiety. Perhaps most important, fatigue erodes subjective standards of performance. As we grow more tired, we are ready to settle for less quality and accuracy. During World War II, Royal Air Force psychologists observed that pilots made the most errors as they drew their planes in for a landing on returning to their base from hazardous raids. The cause, said the analysts, was an "almost irresistible tendency to relax."

Scientists have long tried to isolate the physiological causes of fatigue. They are far from agreement. Some investigations, based for example on treadmill studies, have yielded data on the performance of both the muscular and nervous systems as energy is expended. One set of theories looks to body chemistry measured by the production of lactate in the blood, or a drop in sugar levels (which can often be counteracted quickly, as marathon runners do, with the ingestion of glucose or consumption of large quantities of oxygen). Rest and relaxation are obviously essential.

For most executives, problems of fatigue are probably not physiological. R. F. McFarland, who has conducted studies of people in stressful activities, concludes that "the metabolic cost of mental work is slight." What's most important is usually the emotional fortitude to go the extra distance.

There are those who need an immediate confrontation with failure to provide an extra lift. Edward Uhl, chairman of Fairchild Industries, quotes Archie Moore, the light-heavyweight champion, who was down for a count of nine but went on to win by saying to himself, "If I don't get off the mat, I'll lose the fight." But though a fear of failure can be a goad to action for some people, in others it may serve as a brake. Al Masini, president of TeleRep, has commented that nothing raises the energy reservoir like success, nothing depletes it like failure.

If you find that you tire too quickly, you may want to ask yourself whether you are being worn down by various psychological stresses. Feelings of hostility which must be repressed can consume enormous amounts of psychic energy; you may want to think of letting off steam to a carefully chosen confidant. Chances are you will be tired if you are uncertain what is expected of you, or if you are subject to conflicting expectations; if so, try to straighten out, in your own mind at least, just what you want to achieve. And nothing can be so enervating as boredom; if you are bored look for different work that will stimulate rather than dull your energies.

In extreme cases, psychological fatigue may call for sustained therapy. But the average person who is capable of looking at himself objectively can usually do himself much good by following these principles:

1) Notice particularly what kinds of activity help you relax. Every executive needs to recharge his batteries, and it's important to discover what works best for you. For one individual, it could be music or an art gallery; for others, a steam bath, the golf course or just taking a walk.

2) Keep your sense of humor, which includes your ability to laugh at yourself. In his book "Anatomy of an Illness," Norman Cousins argues as do many physicians that laughter is an invaluable ally in mustering the energy needed to defeat disease. So too, an able business leader knows how to help his group discharge their tension by injecting an appropriate note of levity. Not much is understood about how humor works, but it does seem to relieve stress and to release constructive energies.

3) Acknowledge your areas of dependency. Once we admit that we are not islands of autarchy, and learn to delegate, we can multiply our own resources of stamina by recruiting the strength of others.

If we can acknowledge our need for others as part of our human condition, we can turn to them without feeling guilty or anxious that our dependency is a sign of weakness.

4) Recognize that you have failings as well as virtues—in other words, that you are human. Actually, a knowledge of your limitations can itself provide a source of energy because it tells you where to concentrate. How such a spur can lead to great achievement was illustrated by Somerset Maugham who, at the end of a brilliant writing career, revealed that very early he had discovered his own literary flaws. "I was tired of trying to do what did not come easily to me," he says in his autobiography. He was aware that he had a limited vocabulary, no lyric quality, no gift for metaphor and simile, no imaginative sweep.

"On the other hand," he says, "I had an acute power of observation and it seemed to me that I could see a great many things other people missed. I could put down in clear terms what I saw. I had a logical sense, and if no great feeling for the richness and strangeness of words, at all events a lively appreciation of their sound. I knew that I should never write as well as I could wish, but I thought with pains I could arrive at writing as well as my natural defects allowed."

As with most problems now bedeviling executives, much remains to be learned. We can expect a continuing demand for placebos and fast-cure, over-the-counter remedies. But the ultimate source of a manager's ability to stay the course must be self-discipline. Only then can he share the boast of a genius like Louis Pasteur: "My greatest strength lies solely in my tenacity."

Mr. Feinberg is chairman of BFS Psychological Associates, New York. Mr. Levenstein is professor of management at Baruch College.

Are You Irreplaceable?

By Everett T. Suters

In mechanical systems, it is obvious that parts must be replaceable. A commercial airliner must allow for interchangeability, backup and replaceability. The same is true of management. There must be backup for all parts of the organization. If a manager has people who are irreplaceable, he has not been a good manager.

In the job descriptions of both management and non-management personnel, it should be clearly specified that work should be structured, documented and delegated in such a manner that no one approaches irreplaceability.

Many people in an organization strive to become irreplaceable, erroneously assuming that it will make them more secure in their jobs. This is not the case. It is a paradox of management that if people work at *not* being irreplaceable, they will become more valuable to the organization.

The irreplaceable man represents a logjam to the progression of individuals within an organization. He is a barrier to those under him who want to grow in their jobs.

He is also a nuisance to his superiors. When a person is irreplaceable, problems often become emergencies, and emergencies often become crises. He must sometimes be away from his job, and then responsibilities invariably have to be assumed by a superior, not by someone under him as should be the case. Chief executive officers learn in a hurry to program themselves out of this situation, because there is no one over them who can assume their duties. One bad experience is usually all it takes for a CEO to get his act together.

In small businesses, the boss is often unwilling to delegate, or unable to because of a lack of talent within the organization. Indeed, the syndrome of the irreplaceable boss is a major reason for the high mortality rate of small businesses and the inability of so many of them to grow. Replaceability is often what distinguishes an effective management system from a glorified "candy store operation."

The problem of the "irreplaceable man" is very common, but the solution is simple: vacations. The supervisor of someone who is irreplaceable should give him adequate notice that he is to take a one- or two-week vacation. Up to now, the employee typically will have taken vacations one or two *days* at a time, if at all.

The employee should be told to come up with a plan for covering his responsibilities in his absence. Adequate notice is therefore important, so that the employee has enough time to think through the possible consequences of his taking a vacation and to begin to do something about them. The supervisor should make clear that he will not assume the vacationer's major responsibilities.

There will, of course, be some rough spots during the vacation, and higher management may have to get involved. But it does give higher management the opportunity to find out what is going on and to fix it. When the vacationer returns, he will have a changed job description, with disciplines and controls on the man for his own good, the good of his people and the good of the organization.

Are you irreplaceable? Look for these red flags:

Do you either not take vacations or take them one or two days at a time?

Do you call in constantly while on vacation and try to perform your job long-distance?

Do you try to manage activity instead of managing results?

Are you too busy for your people to talk to you except before or after office hours?

Is there poor morale and a sense of frustration among the people under you?

Are your people not being promoted to higher positions in the organization, or being offered higher positions outside the organization?

Do problems turn into emergencies, and emergencies into crises when you are away?

When you are away, does your superior have to handle your work?

I am not discussing this subject in the abstract. I have been there. I have lived through the agonies of being an irreplaceable man. I have experienced the pressures and anxieties of not being able to feel comfortable away from the office. Only after the job threatened to kill me did I make a conscious decision to program myself out of this situation. Unfortunately, I was a business owner and didn't have anyone to point out the error of my ways or to pressure me into changing my style any sooner.

One of the severest criticisms that can be made of a manager is that he appears to be irreplaceable or that he tolerates irreplaceability among any of his people. A good manager will take whatever steps are necessary to program himself out of this condition.

Mr. Suters is president of Management Services Inc. in Atlanta, and the author of "Succeed in Spite of Yourself" (Van Nostrand Reinhold Co.).

Conversation: The Key to Better Business Writing

By John Louis DiGaetani

Your writing as a manager goes to your subordinates, your colleagues and your superiors. If your memos and business letters make you sound like a pompous illiterate, they may make you the laughing stock of the office.

To avoid this, a useful way to revise your business writing is called the Conversational Test. As you revise, ask yourself if you would ever say to your reader what you are writing. Or imagine yourself speaking to the person instead of writing. If you were talking to a business colleague, would you ever say: "In response to your memo of 11/18/81"? If you did, he would probably laugh.

If you were speaking to a customer, would you ever say: "Enclosed please find your order for three (3) replacement keys"? If you did, your customer would surely think you were weird.

The Conversational Test, while a valid method for revising business writing, is not a mandate for slang. If you were speaking to that colleague, you would maintain a certain formality unless you were friends. If you were speaking to that customer, you might be talking to a total stranger and would certainly not use slang.

But using the Conversational Test will eliminate the mechanical business jargon and cliches that can make your business writing so embarrassing. It will, instead, let your own humanity add color and interest to your writing.

Thus, if you were speaking to a colleague, you would probably say, "I am writing about the question you raised in your last memo." If you were speaking with that customer, you would probably say, "Here are the three replacement keys you ordered." Using the Conversational Test will enable you to write as naturally and persuasively as you speak.

You might imagine a regional sales manager calling up one of his district managers to say, "We don't have the final figures yet for the quarter, but word of mouth has it that they're bad. Inventories are too high again and we might be cutting out some dealerships soon. Just wanted to let you know. I'll send you the figures as soon as I can."

Too often such a person's follow-up memo will read like this: "Re our telephone conversation of July 8, final sales totals for the quarter ending in June are enclosed herewith. A planning conference for all sales personnel will be scheduled for the near future and these figures will be discussed. It is hoped that all district managers will be aware that the figures are such that reductions in the total number of retail units may be indicated. Thank you for your cooperation."

Why does the man who seems so direct and clear on the phone make himself sound mechanical, pompous and stilted in his writing? First, he is probably insecure about his writing skills. He doesn't trust his own use of language enough to write naturally. And he thinks that somehow jargon, wordy expressions, the passive voice and puffy sentences will make him appear more educated or more polished than he fears he really is. Second, he may be under the impression that business writing is supposed to seem stuffy, roundabout and impersonal since so many of the memos he gets read that way. Finally, he may be timid about putting certain information—in this case bad news—too bluntly, especially in writing.

All of these reasons are equally bad. Chances are your command of English is plenty good enough if you just write things down as naturally as you say them. Trying to puff things up and give added heft to your everyday thoughts only makes you seem like a blowhard. It impresses only the naive. Lots of business people adopt such a stilted style when writing, but the truly savvy are not impressed.

And direct, clear writing which approximates the way reasonable people speak will never embarrass you. Trying to hide bad news in a fog of wordiness just doesn't work. The reader of the memo cited above, once he manages to figure out its content, is going to be annoyed and maybe amused. If you're the writer, you might as well state your message as simply and clearly as you can and spare your reader the added burdens of trying to puzzle out its meaning. And the Conversational Test will help you here.

But one warning: The test will work best if your parents did not speak a foreign language or a dialect of English at home. If you did not learn standard American English at home, you will have to be more careful to revise according to the rules of grammar and usage.

But for most business people, the key to better writing is as close as their mouths. Using the Conversational Test will vastly improve the quality of their business writing. It will make their writing as interesting and human as they are.

Mr. DiGaetani teaches English at Hofstra University.

Improving Your Alertness

By Robert D. Reid

I read "The Management of Time" by James T. McCay (Prentice-Hall, 176 pages, $14.95, paperback $4.95) in 1959, the year it came out. Since then I've read and reread it, corresponded and met with its author, forced the book on friends and sent copies to interested business acquaintances. I'm not alone. "The Management of Time" has been one of the all-time best-sellers for a business non-textbook— 300,000 copies, mostly hardcover, have been sold.

There are several reasons for the book's enthusiastic reception. It is slim. It is simply written. It uses interesting examples and analogies. Most important, it appeals to the multitude of managers who find themselves under so much time pressure that they can't find time for the things they think are most important. Along comes an author who declares they can increase their effectiveness in using time by leaps and bounds. He does this with more conviction than the dozens of other authors who have written books on the same subject.

A jump in effectiveness is necessary, Mr. McCay states, because the tempo and the complexity of business have also jumped. There are more and bigger problems than in the past. Every year more new ideas are created and applied sooner. He illustrates with this example: "Gunpowder was invented in the 12th century, but it was not applied in warfare until 200 years later. Atomic fission was first observed in 1939 and applied within five years. Ratio: Forty to one."

"Faced with a mushrooming workload that you can neither cut down nor delegate, you need more than time-saving techniques," Mr. McCay insists. His central thesis is that managers can multiply their effectiveness by increasing their alertness, building up their available energy and broadening their knowledge, as well as by applying some skills of managing time. The goal is to "increase the size of the pipes" rather than to raise the pressure by working still harder over still longer hours.

Mr. McCay contends that managers would be much more effective if they simply paid more attention to what is going on around them and to the tasks at hand. To heighten alertness, he suggests changing routines. "Throughout the day, ...flicker your attention over the many facets of what is going on about you." Have a daily practice session: For example, work on tone, inflection and gesticulation in giving a speech. And cultivate at least one interest centering on observation, such as hunting galaxies with a telescope.

If you don't have the energy to apply time-saving techniques, there is little reason to acquire them. Mr. McCay stresses the importance of storing energy and shielding yourself from energy losses. In particular, he advises managers not to be critical of others in their organizations, and not to be defensive whenever someone suggests they might do things differently. Both, he suggests, can be tremendous drains of energy, and he recommends that managers check in with themselves several times a day to make sure they aren't silently stewing about some imagined slight.

With respect to broadening knowledge, Mr. McCay stresses the importance of making more and better mental pictures, and making them faster. One way to do this is to explore new ideas, and Mr. McCay encourages the time-short manager to pick up as many informative books as he can. It isn't necessary, he claims, to read books all the way through; on the contrary, many of them aren't worth the effort. But he recommends that busy managers read at least the first few paragraphs of each chapter, then decide if it's worth burrowing more deeply.

Another way to make more mental pictures is to explore new sensory experiences. Eat new foods, go to new places. The author is convinced that many opportunities for boosting effectiveness lie in the unfamiliar. Using the analogy of a radar-electronic computer installation, he states: "When you explore the world of ideas you increase the capacity of your computer...when you explore new sensations you increase the sensitivity and range of your antennae... [broadening, respectively] your 'know-about'...[and] your 'know-how'."

Mr. McCay devotes a chapter each to seven specific skills for managing time more efficiently. Two examples are diagramming and using analogies, both of which can dramatically cut down the time you need to communicate ideas to your associates. Drawing a diagram on a blackboard or easel pad, he asserts, can often communicate abstract ideas much more quickly than the usual cross-the-table discussion. And he argues that "one good analogy is often worth three hours' discussion." I recall years ago how an abstract concept, the experiential obsolescence of older managers, came alive to me from one of Mr. McCay's analogies: "He is like the Second World War bomber pilot who can no longer qualify for air crew because his experience doesn't apply to the new jet bombers."

A very simple piece of advice is to list on a slip of paper those tasks that we *have to* do today, and those that we *should do* today. Then *do* the tasks on the first slip one by one, while filing away for future reference the second slip. It is amazing how much this simple system can release one from time pressure.

"The Management of Time" is a major contribution because of the importance of its subject, the originality and conviction behind its suggestions and the appealing writing style of its author.

Mr. Reid is an executive search consultant in Chicago.

That Feeling in Your Bones: When to Rely on Your Intuition?

By Mortimer R. Feinberg and
Aaron Levenstein

"I just feel it in my gut!"

With those words the chief executive officer (CEO) brushes aside the unanimous recommendation of his subordinates. He disregards the data they cite—market surveys, past sales performance, interviews with customers—and decides to stick with a faltering product. And, despite all the logic on the other side, he turns out to be right.

Albert Einstein attributed his theory of relativity to a flash of insight, not to the cold rationalism of the objective, data-oriented researcher in the laboratory. True, his mind had been prepared by much study and thought, but as he said later, "The really valuable factor is intuition."

So, too, in business, decisions based on shrewd intuition are often superior to those based on careful analytical reasoning. Charles Revson, the builder of Revlon, seemed to have an uncanny knack for determining what the consumer would want. Jack Chamberlin, now chairman of Lenox and formerly with General Electric, recalls his decision about whether to go with an eight-track or cassette tape, in the early days of the technology. One offered better fidelity; the other, greater convenience to users. Deciding to "go by gut," he opted for the latter, an intuition that proved right.

Defining intuition isn't easy. Some executives call it "a

feeling in my bones," guesstimate, speculation, imagination, creativity. William C. Shanley III, president of Amstar Corp.'s American Sugar Division, resists the term "hunch," saying it is unrelated to intuition. He thinks hunches suggest a mechanical process, like the gambler playing the horse that has the same name as a favorite aunt.

Nor is intuition to be confused with impulsiveness. The latter is simply a rush to judgment, often motivated by plain laziness or a desire to avoid the facts. Intuitiveness, on the other hand, welcomes data even though it refuses to be limited to it. Einstein, informed by his intuitions, nevertheless contrived a series of tests and experiments to prove or disprove his insights.

Recent studies of the brain suggest that the left hemisphere is the locus of our logical, sequential, rational and verbal processes, while the right side is the organ for intuitive, imaginative, artistic and creative processes. Despite all the attention given to "rationalism" in management literature and education, a study by Harry Mintzberg of McGill University has suggested that CEOs in leading companies actually use the right side—the intuitive hemisphere—in about 80% of their decisions.

A number of CEOs told us they rely on intuition primarily in hiring, placing and promoting people. Others say they apply it in product decisions, particularly in fashion and entertainment industries. On the other hand, some executives, such as Robert A. M. Coppenrath, president and general manager of Agfa-Gevaert, insist that intuition must be reined in. "It seems to work better as an alarm, a warning system, than as a trigger for action," he says. "As far as I am concerned, it commands better nonaction than action."

Intuition, of course, can lead to just as many mistakes as rational logic can. By definition, creative intuition cannot be the product of a formula. But certain questions are useful in determining whether your "gut feeling" is worth following:

Ask yourself if you are influenced by wishful thinking and pure guesswork. James Cook, president of L.G. Balfour, says he differentiates between "gut and guess" by observing his own reactions to what occurs when his colleagues are shooting down his ideas. If his feeling persists, "and gnaws and gnaws and gnaws," he is more likely to stay with his intuition.

Is your intuitive conclusion based on what psychologists call selective perception? Do you want to keep alive a dying product simply because you have pride of authorship, or do you have some basis for your intuition? Do you want to sell off a successful product simply because it bores you?

Is your conclusion due, not to intuition but to mental rigidity? That is, are you reacting by habit or a desire to vindicate past policy, refusing to recognize that a change has occurred in the environment? One of the problems with the U.S. auto and steel industries may have been that executives relied too much on their "feel" for the business, rather than paying attention to what their competitors around the world were doing.

Has your judgment been affected by your personal inclinations, for instance a tendency to be optimistic or pessimistic? Are you allowing a flood of emotion to drown good sense? The classic case is that of the British businessman who continued to make a money-losing product because Buckingham Palace was still buying it, even though the general public had turned thumbs down on it.

Can you set up a trial run and avoid a premature, irrevocable commitment? The general who "feels" that the enemy's lines are overextended might want to launch probing maneuvers before he throws his full forces into battle. Intuition must be constantly monitored and tested. Indeed, one of its advantages, according to Richard Brown, former president of Towle Manufacturing Co., is that "when following intuition, you develop a natural tendency to stay closer to the decision and audit it earlier and more often than in decisions based on hard reasoning."

The key question is the one that troubled Joan of Arc: The inner voices may be loud and clear, but do they come from heaven or hell?

The ultimate safeguard is to avoid stubbornness, to listen sympathetically to what others say and to subject all decisions, whether the fruits of reason or of intuition, to searching examination.

Mr. Feinberg is chairman of BFS Psychological Associates, a New York consulting firm. Mr. Levenstein is professor emeritus, management, Baruch College.

Public Speaking

By Ralph Proodian

Top executives, and those who hope to be at or near the top, need to know how to prepare and read a speech. They cannot take chances with outlines, because one slip can result in more than embarrassment. Success depends on correct preparation and skilled delivery.

Reading aloud must not degenerate into saying words as they appear on the page. When we write, we separate words to identify them. But spoken words must be linked together as syllables are linked. When you run words together, as you do in normal conversational speaking, you develop fluency and, believe it or not, clarity. As we rarely express an idea in a word, groups of words or phrases must be perceived as single units. The way to do this is by linking the words of a phrase, saying them in an uninterrupted flow of air. The trick is to say the last sound of each word *as if* (i.e. azif) it is the first sound of the next word. Your meaning will then be easier to follow.

If you are skeptical, try saying the words in this sentence one at a time just as they appear on the page. You will see how that pace is both dull and difficult to sustain. If you recite word lists, the listener will turn you off.

We also can stretch and shrink words when we say them, which we cannot do in writing. Note that words like "from," "shall" and "there" are longer on the page than "run," "pen" and "coal," but are less important. In speaking, you can reveal the relative importance of words by the amount of time you give them. To weaken words you must say them so quickly that their vowel sounds are almost eliminated.

While preparing your text, keep the following points in mind and you will have a special advantage:

Know the difference between words in writing and in talking. They are not the same. Consider: "Since you are aware of the difficulties involved in the project..." vs. this spoken version, "Since you know how hard this job will be...." And again, "I am fully aware of your critical role in this acquisition..." vs. "I know this takeover wouldn't have worked without you...." Words like "participation," "obstinacy" and even "evaluate" are not as good in speech as "work," "stubbornness" and "consider." Stick to words normally used in daily conversation. Unless, of course, you swear a lot.

Read aloud to get the feeling of the words flowing out of your mouth. Pay attention to your meaning. Be sure you emphasize nouns and verbs, not prepositions and other helpers. Most people, for example, say: "Give it *to* me"—the least meaningful emphasis. Any of these would be better: "*Give* it to me," or "Give *it* to me," or "Give it to *me.*"

Sentence length is critical. Long sentences, balanced with carefully thought-out qualifying phrases containing subtle points, can be reread and studied but are not easy to follow through the ear. Nonetheless, long spoken sentences are generally understood easily as long as they are not packed with very many details. Conversation is looser than writing because we back up and fill in and clarify as we interact. The continual feedback of conversation is missing in writing and reading.

Short sentences, in fact, are generally a virtue in writing but a problem in speaking. When the music in speech is eliminated by terse, staccato sentences, we resist listening. The music of speaking, like the Pied Piper's flute, seduces us to listen. But, of course, too much of a good thing.... The bottom line is that you should be able to speak the sentences as easily as you would in normal conversation.

25

Preparing the manuscript: Wide margins, quadruple spacing of lines—lots of space all around. Use the space to make notes of minor points or appropriate anecdotes to be included parenthetically. One speaker I know makes such notes and ad-libs the short digressions as a way of injecting spontaneity into his reading.

I am uncomfortable with everything in capital letters. The beginnings of sentences are hard to recognize. Periods are not under enough pressure; they seem too small.

Even if you haven't the time to write it yourself, put some of yourself into your speech. Find a speech writer you like and work with him exclusively. He will get to know your values and sense of humor, how you use words, and how you structure sentences and speak them. He will be able to imagine your intonations, rhythms and ways of emphasizing important points. In short, he will capture you in his early drafts. The speech you read, therefore, will be *your* speech—not just *a* speech.

Practice without mirrors, video recordings or audio tapings. I know this advice flies in the face of popular opinion. But you are better off without them. Seeming spontaneity and naturalness is what you need. Any device that makes you self-conscious undermines that goal. Turn your attention away from yourself and to your audience. Those in the audience will express their appreciation by listening.

Always be aware of what you are saying and your voice will be as expressive as you can make it. If you have a nasal twang or monotone, a strong regional or foreign accent, a minor diction problem such as a lisp, or a raspy or hoarse voice due to strain, do something about them—but not on the eve of giving a speech. Those long-term problems should be taken care of eventually if you are going to represent your company well.

Finally, have your wife or husband give your speech its final check. Unlike your well-meaning colleagues, neither will be shy about telling you the truth.

Mr. Proodian is a New York-based speech consultant and coach.

The Workaholic Boss: An 18-Hour-a-Day Menace

By Jack Falvey

The biggest problem with trying to manage stress in organizations is that we try to do just that, manage it, instead of getting rid of the people who are causing all the stress in the first place. It really is pointless to recommend relaxation response periods, deep breathing exercises and other "stress-reduction" techniques when the carriers of the malady are breathing fire just around the corner.

I'm talking about the so-called workaholic manager—a contradiction in terms, because if you're a workaholic, you can't be a manager. A workaholic placed in a management position, and that's usually where he ends up, is one of the most divisive forces roaming the corridors of the industrialized world.

Just think about the contradictions involved. Where a manager must set priorities, the workaholic must do everything. (This also occurs on a temporary basis for start-up entrepreneurs. Within a short time, they usually learn to do only what is important.)

A manager must be patient in gaining the commitment of others, in order to multiply his efforts. The workaholic has little or no patience with others and works unending hours to make up for their perceived lack of commitment. This creates the self-fulfilling prophecy of only being able to rely on his own work.

Where a manager negotiates objectives and time frames for accomplishment, the workaholic sets arbitrary deadlines and then applies follow-up pressure to assure compliance. He often is rewarded with malevolent obedience, usually with shoddy results.

I wish the following example were not true. While attending a three-day management meeting at a resort hotel, a junior staff member approached his boss during an after-dinner cocktail party. His objective was to see if he could ride back on the plane with the boss on the following day and discuss his next six-months' support plans. Repeated previous attempts to get a meeting date had failed. The ever cheerful high-energy boss said that he already had an in-flight meeting scheduled but, "No problem, let's step into the next room and go over the plans right now." And so at 12:45 a.m. the subordinate did his best to make an orderly presentation of the plans and objectives of his department for the next six months.

Any manager who behaves like that is an "18-hour-a-day-menace," who carries stress wherever he goes.

He arrives early and leaves late. He sends a message that this is the standard of behavior expected. Since most people can't follow his leadership, he breeds resentment and antagonism.

The lunch at the desk and scheduling of every working hour further cut off conversation, commitment and contributions of others.

There is no doubt, of course, that companies need dedicated employees who put in long hours and love attention to detail. It just has to be remembered that this is not necessarily the type of person you want to be in charge of gaining the quality commitment of others. The biggest, strongest worker has not historically made the best foreman, even though that was often the promotion policy.

How about finding some nice staff projects for your workaholics, so they can immerse themselves in the incredible detail they love?

Direct their high energy levels to tasks, not the management of people.

Just stop and think about all the workaholic "war stories" you have heard. Think about the running through airports, about the two meetings going on at once, about the lines waiting outside of "executive" offices trying to get on the schedule, about the blizzard of phone messages generated around these so-called managers. Many organizations and people are resilient enough to succeed in spite of this type of direction. But survival should not be the standard of performance.

So do what you can to reduce the stress level in your organization to reasonable operational levels. Do it by keeping the workaholic out of the management function. Control and concentrate energy into the most compact and narrow areas possible in order to do the most important things best and to reward the best people with the business leadership they deserve. Come and go at reasonable hours. Families all throughout your organization will be forever grateful. Don't confuse high energy levels with the brainpower necessary to produce results.

If you are a manager think about your effect on others. They are the ones who must produce the results that you are judged on. Are you a workaholic in a management position? Are you reading this at 5:30 a.m. or midnight? Have two or three people sent you this article? Have 10 people sent it to you?

Mr. Falvey is a management consultant based in Londonderry, N.H.

Making Positive Things Happen

By Ralph Z. Sorenson

Years ago, when I was a young assistant professor at the Harvard Business School, I thought that the key to developing managerial leadership lay in raw brain power. I thought the role of business schools was to develop future managers who knew all about the various functions of business; to teach them how to define problems succinctly, analyze these problems and identify alternatives in a clear, logical fashion, and, finally, to teach them to make an intelligent decision.

My thinking gradually became tempered by living and working outside the U.S. and by serving seven years as a college president. During my presidency of Babson College, I added several additional traits or skills that I felt a good manager must possess.

The first is the *ability to express oneself* in a clear, articulate fashion. Good oral and written communication skills are absolutely essential if one is to be an effective manager.

Second, one must possess that amorphous and intangible set of qualities called *leadership skills*. To be a good leader one must understand and be sensitive to people and be able to inspire them toward the achievement of common goals.

Next I concluded that effective managers must be *broad human beings* who not only understand the world of busi-

30

ness but also have a sense of the cultural, social, political, historical and (particularly today) the international aspects of life and society. This suggests that exposure to the liberal arts and humanities should be part of every manager's education.

Finally, as I pondered the lessons of Watergate and the almost daily litany of business and government-related scandals that have occupied the front pages of newspapers throughout the '70s and early '80s, it became abundantly clear that a good manager in today's world must have *courage and a strong sense of integrity*. He or she must know where to draw the line between right and wrong.

That can be agonizingly difficult. Drawing a line in a corporate setting sometimes involves having to make a choice between what appears at first glance to be conflicting "rights." For example, if one is faced with a decision whether to close an ailing factory, whose interests should prevail? Stockholders? Employees? Customers? Or those of the community in which the factory is located? It's a tough choice. And the typical manager faces many others.

Sometimes, these choices involve simple questions of honesty or truthfulness. More often, they are more subtle and involve such issues as having to decide whether to "cut corners" to meet "bottom line" profit objectives that may be expedient in the short run, but that are not in the best long-term interests of the various constituencies being served by one's company. Making the right choice in situations such as these clearly demands integrity and the courage to follow where one's integrity leads.

But now I have shed the cap and gown of a college president and donned the hat of chief executive officer. As a result of my experience as a corporate CEO, my list of desirable managerial traits has become still longer.

It now seems to me that what matters most in the majority of organizations is to have reasonably intelligent, hard-working managers who have a sense of pride and loyalty toward their organization; who can get to the root of a problem and are inclined toward action; who are decent human beings with a natural empathy and concern for people; who possess humor, humility and common sense; and who are able to couple drive with stick-to-it-iveness and patience in the accomplishment of a goal.

It is the *ability to make positive things happen* which most distinguishes the successful manager from the mediocre or unsuccessful one. It is far better to have dependable managers who can make the right things happen in a timely fashion than to have brilliant, sophisticated, highly educated executives who are excellent at planning, analyzing and dissecting, but who are not so good at implementing. The most cherished manager is the one who says "I can do it," and then does.

Many business schools continue to focus almost exclusively on the development of analytical skills. As a result, these schools are continuing to graduate legions of MBA's and business majors who know a great deal about analyzing strategies, dissecting balance sheets and using computers— but who still don't know how to manage!

Business schools should be encouraged to refashion their curricula to place more emphasis on helping students realize the vital importance of supplementing analytical and decision-making skills with the additional character traits, leadership skills and good old-fashioned management virtues that lie at the very core of effective management.

As a practical matter, of course, schools can go only so far in teaching their students to manage. Only hard knocks and actual work experience will fully develop and hone the kinds of managerial traits, skills and virtues that I have discussed here.

Put another way: The best way to learn to manage is to manage. Companies such as mine that hire aspiring young managers can help the process along by:

—providing good role models and mentors;

—setting clear standards and high expectations which emphasize the kind of broad-gauged leadership traits that are important to the organization, and then rewarding young managers accordingly; and

—letting young managers actually manage.

Having thereby encouraged those who are not only "the

best and the brightest" but *also* broad, sensitive human beings possessing all of the other traits and virtues essential for true managerial leadership to rise to the top, we just might be able to breathe a bit more easily about the future health of industry and society.

Mr. Sorenson is president and chief executive officer of Barry Wright Corp., a manufacturer of computer related accessories and other diversified industrial products.

Paying Your Dues

By Frank R. Beaudine

Three decades ago general consulting was still a relatively young profession, not quite as polished and refined as it is today, but growing at a rapid pace. Consultants as a group were older, since the now-common practice of moving directly from graduate school to consulting was just beginning.

Even then, McKinsey & Co. was a well-known and highly respected firm. It was a sophisticated company, moving boldly on important assignments "from the top management point of view," and was inhabited by professionals with undergraduate and graduate degrees from prestigious universities. Marketing and finance were their primary areas of expertise.

Due to rapid growth demands and a desire to have a more broadly based staff, McKinsey decided to recruit some people with practical operating experience. And so, in 1956 or thereabouts, armed only with a degree from a Midwestern university and 10 years of industrial-engineering experience with one company, I burst upon the scene as a McKinsey associate in its Chicago office.

I have to tell you—it took me quite awhile to get the hang of it.

First of all, I was woefully lacking in consultanese. "Optimizing" and "maximizing" were just words to me, instead of concepts everyone else seemed to grasp easily and vocalize glibly. The majority of my peers had MBAs from what they called the "B" school. It was some time before I discovered they were talking about Harvard.

During my first month or so on the job I read one of Peter Drucker's early books on management and, filled with new and exciting concepts, I tried to impress one of the principals of the firm with my newly acquired in-depth thinking. He listened for a bit and then commented, "Peter is droll, isn't he?"

Another problem I had was that most of my colleagues seemed far ahead of me in general business know-how. As a result, my insecurities grew, and one manifestation of this was to try to make sense out of business conversations and to leap in at odd moments with what I hoped were brilliant comments. They were generally followed by brief lulls, and then the conversations would resume without acknowledgement.

My most compelling sense of awe, however, was reserved for the firm's managing director, Marvin Bower. Marvin personified McKinsey to me and his least utterance was like a proclamation from the mountaintop. When Marvin said "Good morning," he really meant it. I mean, it broke down. It was, first of all, unquestionably "morning." Not only that, but it was a "GOOD" morning. I could generally list at least four major and six minor reasons for it being "good," and sometimes there even were subminor reasons.

Marvin was a big man, lean and rugged. His eyes were steely and flashed brilliantly. His deep resonant voice commanded attention and respect.

Marvin set the tone for McKinsey—professional, dignified and sophisticated. This was accomplished in part by written guidelines. For every part of a consulting assignment there were guidelines. Writing a client report, for example, was a major subject for coverage. It had to "stand the test of time." I used to dread the thought of some executives of the future coming across one of my reports and one saying to another, "Poor chap. His report simply didn't stand the test of time."

The managing director of our Chicago office liked the reports to "zing" him. He would glance over one of mine and shake his head sadly. "I think I see what you mean," he might say, "but it just doesn't zing me." I must confess that in my few years with McKinsey I never did actually zing him—a small tingle now and then perhaps, but never a real zing.

In addition to guidelines, Marvin also had "Rules." These related more to conduct and appearance. Never discuss a client's business on an elevator, for example. Always wear a hat. Perhaps most important, always wear garters. Marvin and, presumably, clients were appalled if you crossed your legs and drooping socks or bare skin appeared.

We used to have Saturday morning training in those days—four-hour meetings to advance our consulting skills rather than our golf or tennis. From time to time, Marvin made an appearance at those meetings; when he did, he would usually take command, set up some sort of problem and lead the discussion. These were not good times for me.

I remember once he started out, "This past week I was in London..."

Wow. I had been spending all my time in and around Chicago and here Marvin had been in London. Thinking about this caused me to miss some of the problem he was constructing. Suddenly Marvin was pointing at me. "What three key business elements are involved in that instance and how do they relate to our clients?"

I was still marveling that Marvin had been in London yesterday and here in Chicago today and mumbled something to the effect that since I'd never been in England I couldn't come to grips with the problem. This brought chuckles and condescending glances from the rest of the group and led some to conclude I was a smart aleck.

Well, time rolled on, and after a couple of years I left McKinsey and returned to industry. A few years later I was on board the Broadway Limited, and when I went to have breakfast, who was seated at the same table but Marvin Bower.

It was somewhat of a shock.

First of all, Marvin wasn't all that big. And he wasn't lean. In fact, slightly portly might better describe him. His eyes didn't glare, but were warm and friendly. The deep voice was actually pleasant and well modulated.

As I was recovering from this set of surprises, I noticed he had cut himself shaving and had a little piece of the paper we all use for that sort of thing stuck on his chin. The general impact of all this was a bit disconcerting.

It was an interesting breakfast. I found out that Marvin was reasonably aware of the work I had done at McKinsey and was also aware of my current career progress. As I chatted with this intelligent, friendly man I realized that, of course, he had not changed—but I had. My time at McKinsey had been meaningful and, on balance, enjoyable. My parting had been amicable and in fact, the McKinsey people were most helpful in my successful relocation.

In subsequent years the value of my McKinsey period has been further impressed upon me. In my own business, the background gained in problem solving, organizational planning and client relationships has been a major asset.

It occurred to me even then, however, that in one form or another most business executives have their "McKinsey" experience—a sharp upward learning curve that can cause some consternation at the time but is in reality a dues-paying experience that is essential for real growth.

Mr. Beaudine is chairman of Eastman & Beaudine Inc., an international executive search firm based in Chicago.

Beware of the Business Lunch

By Martin H. Bauman

Too often the business lunch is an unproductive ritual we perform during the business day, more because it's expected than because it's efficient.

Public settings are inappropriate for serious business, such as high-level negotiations. Confidential conversations are hampered by surrounding noises and eavesdroppers. Restaurants also obscure the subtle changes of voice, body language and facial codes that are so important in judging a partner's reactions to what you say. It is difficult to observe these changes when half the body is hidden.

"People are more practiced in lying with their words than with faces, and more practiced with faces than with body movements," writes Paul Ekman, a University of California psychology professor, in "Unmasking the Face." "When listening, you gather information from actual words used, the sound of the voice, and such things as how rapidly words are spoken."

There also are visual messages: "the face, the tilts of the head, the total body posture and the skeletal muscle movements of the arms, hands, legs, and feet." That strained expression on a luncheon partner's face may be the strain of hearing you. His relaxed body language, on the other hand, may be a trained response to a social setting that hides a revealing tension that would be apparent if he were sitting in an office chair.

Lunches put too much of a premium on social skills. Ease in a restaurant discloses nothing more than a certain kind of conditioning. It tells nothing about acuity or creativity. Indeed, some gifted executives have absolutely no small talk; at times they may appear socially retarded. In an office, however, the emotional mechanism shifts gears and they operate at 100%.

Restaurants may make people too comfortable. A skilled negotiator, for example, watches for response time. "I threw out a number and he didn't even blink," remembers one executive. Taking a bite, sipping a drink and calling for the waiter all can be effective stalls.

The ambiance of restaurants sometimes makes them unsuitable for business meetings when the ability to talk and react freely is vital. There are times, for instance, when anger is an appropriate response, something that isn't possible in public hearing and in public view. This is especially the case where industries tend to gather geographically. Nearby, the table may be filled with executives from a competing company.

Next, consider the cost of luncheons. Including travel, lunching usually consumes two to 2½ hours of the standard 10-hour executive workday. That is as much as 25%. Two top-level officers compensated at, say, $200 an hour, spend $1,000 by lunching. And that doesn't include the price of what is usually an expensive meal.

That may be petty cash in million-dollar contracts, but is it an efficient use of money? In fact, it usually is not. Most often, the real deal-making takes place back in the office. One client, a general partner in a major investment banking concern, sums up the common misconception: "The fellow who thinks I'm 'friendlier' over lunch than in my office is naive."

But what about friendliness? Does lunching have a valid purpose in creating personal empathies? Under certain conditions it does.

Lunching is useful when interpersonal exchanges are necessary. Some industries feed on human connections. "In advertising," says the president of one major agency, "personal chemistry with the client is very important. Rapport and the establishment of a good relationship are the key. A meal has no entertainment value. We're really communicating."

Other companies or industries also use lunch as working time. According to the executive vice president of a cosmetics company: "Lunches between division heads are a way of life here. During the business day, the people you want to talk with are busy running their functions. Lunch is the only place to get things done."

Too often, however, executives fail to recognize that meeting for lunch is just like any other conference; there must be an agenda. The key, says one client, is to ask yourself, "What would be the best possible outcome of this lunch?" and then to block out the plan formally on a piece of paper. Treated this way, it's possible to avoid one of the perils of lunch: the unconscious dribbling away of time in a relaxed social setting.

Lunching is useful in other ways. Within companies it can provide a casual setting that often circumvents the negative results of in-office confrontations. And, for new employees, lunch with colleagues tends to hasten the integration process.

Finally, there is one occasion for which lunching has indisputable advantages that cannot easily be duplicated. Recently we were called upon to bring together two high-powered corporate stars. An office visit of one to the other would have been an insupportable loss of face. Arranging a luxurious lunch—meeting on a first-class neutral ground—prevented that. Here, the social occasion helped avoid a power struggle: Neither executive had to give anything away.

There are, thus, occasions when lunch is an effective tool. However, it's always necessary to remember that the main purpose of a business lunch is business. Its only effective use is when, by lunching, an executive eventually "feeds" his company a deal.

Mr. Bauman is president of Martin H. Bauman Associates, a New York recruiting firm.

The Art of Constructive Procrastination

By Ross A. Webber

One of the keys to effective time management is knowing when to procrastinate.

There are some decisions—especially such personnel actions as hiring, firing, promoting, transferring and evaluating staff—where slow, deliberate decision-making helps to avoid mistakes down the road. As Gypsy Rose Lee once observed in another context, "Anything worth doing well is worth doing slowly."

Then there are times when a subordinate has an obligation to put off doing what a superior demands, in order to protect the boss from the consequences of his own folly.

Furious at a "Huntley-Brinkley" report, President Kennedy once ordered the chairman of the Federal Communications Commission, Newton Minow, to punish NBC through any means available. Mr. Minow did nothing, then wrote Kennedy indicating how lucky he was to have subordinates too loyal to always do as they were told. Kennedy agreed when his anger abated.

Sometimes it's essential to say "no" to the boss when time demands are excessive. The worst sin a manager could commit at ITT under Harold Geneen was not to warn the chairman that a task could not be completed by his desired date. This failure to confront the boss was even worse than being late.

Perhaps most important is knowing what minor jobs can safely be deferred in order to free up time for the really important tasks.

One hesitates to use President Richard Nixon as an example of good management. Nonetheless, he was an effective time scheduler. To free blocks of time, he would leave the White House and walk across the street to the Executive Office Building, where he maintained a hide-away office. Once he was there with his yellow legal pads, the staff knew he was to be interrupted only for true emergencies. Nixon could therefore focus on the big issues.

The office of Senator McClure of Idaho has experimented with a form of enforced procrastination called "quiet hours." During this period, all incoming telephone calls are blocked by a switchboard with a promise that the desired person will return the call at a certain time, no visitors are scheduled, no telephone calls are initiated, and internal office communication or meetings are discouraged. People are free to think about the ambiguous and creative tasks.

Constructive procrastination can take more modest forms, too. For example, never do business during lunch that can be put off until the afternoon. Business lunches eat into your free time. Medical research supports skipping the working lunch in favor of eating alone because debating while eating is one of the most stressful executive activities.

The effective manager, of course, also must know when to complete the important tasks. If you're having trouble finishing those jobs that matter most, here are some tips:

Set beginning times. This may appear to be a delaying tactic, but not every task can be started immediately. Enter a date and time on your calendar.

Generate momentum. Starting with easy, programmed tasks like routine correspondence and bureaucratic detail can lead you into the tougher jobs you can't start first thing in the morning or after lunch. But set a desk alarm clock for 30 minutes and give up those tasks to confront the ambiguous.

Reward yourself for progress. All complex projects have smaller parts that can be celebrated as they are completed.

A coffee break or even an afternoon off to play golf are justified if they follow the actual work.

Include others in rewards. One sad aspect of modern work life is that it is divorced from family life. Children and spouses may not even know when you have accomplished something significant on the job; so give yourself a small gift that can be shared with them. Thank them for their implicit support of your work.

Set deadlines earlier than necessary. Effective time managers seldom accept other people's deadlines, but create earlier, artificial ones that give them more control and ease the harriedness of the last-minute rush. They—and you—can act upon time before it can pass by.

When you were a child, did you eat your spinach first or last? Many of us had parents who enforced a rule allowing "no dessert" until all of the main course was eaten, including the dreaded vegetable. Procrastinators seem to put off "eating their spinach" in hope that the demanding parent— or boss—will relax his guard and forget to enforce the rule. In contrast, non-procrastinators usually consume the spinach of their job first.

Good luck, and *bon appétit.*

Mr. Webber is vice president for development and alumni relations at the University of Pennsylvania, and professor of management at the Wharton School. He is the author of "Time Is Money." This article is adapted from The Wharton Magazine.

2

Technology

Steel Collar Workers: How to Use Robots

By Kenichi Ohmae

Japan leads the world in robot use and production and its enthusiasm for robotics has been widely reported. What hasn't yet received much attention are the strategic implications for management that can be drawn from Japanese experience.

Lesson number one is that robots will shake up the structure of industries where labor accounts for a significant portion of manufacturing costs. For tasks such as welding, painting and even many assembly operations, reasonably sophisticated robots working two shifts a day will soon pay for themselves in less than a year. In this environment, companies relying on labor will be extremely vulnerable to competition from companies which have switched much of their manufacturing process to robots. For example, American and European semiconductor manufacturers that rely on labor-intensive processes in low-wage countries have fallen behind in integrated circuit/LSI market share, as companies, such as Nippon Electric, have withdrawn production from scattered sites in Southeast Asia and consolidated it in highly automated Japanese plants.

Second, robots provide recession resistance. Anticipating high volatility in their mature domestic markets and uncertainties in their export markets, Japanese blue chip companies are trying to build operations that will make money at anything over 70% capacity. They are finding that robots, which can work many shifts, are the key to lowering break-even points.

Toyota Motors has publicly announced it has achieved the 70% goal. Fujitsu-Fanuc, the world leader in numerically controlled machines, claims that its plant at Fuji-oshino Mura breaks even at 30% utilization. These plants are extremely resilient in downturns. While competitors suffer from operating losses and sleepless nights worrying about layoffs and union resistance, robot-run plants can simply switch to one-shift operation.

Third, robots reduce barriers to entry. One of the most fascinating aspects of robotics in Japan is that many smaller manufacturers are taking the lead in installing sophisticated robots.

What robots do is help smaller companies enter precision machinery, fabrication and assembly industries, from which they had previously been barred because of a shortage of skilled workers. Sophisticated robots can carry out complex machining, welding, assembly and other skilled operations with flawless and tireless accuracy. Unlike traditional automation, which tended to replace simple manual workers, robots can replace experienced and skilled workers. Thus a small entrepreneurial corporation can now challenge the status quo and labor-intensive approaches of old-fashioned incumbents that have built up a skilled work force over the years. Pentel, which is aggressively stealing shares of the global pen market, is an example of a small company that has broken into the market by using sophisticated assembly robots.

Fourth, robots greatly increase manufacturing flexibility. The availability of high quality labor, for example, used to be one of the primary factors in determining where to locate a plant. With robots, managers no longer face that constraint, and they can choose plant sites in order to minimize logistics and transportation costs, attract first-class management talent or do almost anything that will give the company a strategic edge.

Robots give companies greater freedom to meet different specifications for a given product line. Reduction in a stamping machine's changeover time from 45 to two minutes has enabled Toyota to eliminate the traditional worry of optimum lot size. In fact, robots are helping Japanese automakers shift the basis of their competitive strategy from price to fashion.

Similarly, robots have helped Japanese plain paper copier makers introduce new models more quickly, and are giving Japanese consumer electronics companies a substantial lead in industries that are moving fast into fashion. One such company can ship out a new model color TV less than half a year after receiving specifications from the marketing department. Casio in calculators, Sony in portable cassettes and Konica in 35mm lens-shutter cameras, all use short turnaround time to shake out slow moving contenders by accelerating model life cycles.

The fifth and probably most important lesson from Japanese experience is that companies can benefit from robots only if they take great care in preparing for their introduction.

Management must make sure, for example, that it doesn't alienate workers and unions. Even in Japan, worker resistance has stymied robot introduction in cases where workers felt that robots were taking away the pleasant and easy jobs, leaving dirty and unpleasant work for people. Where robots have replaced people in hostile working environments such as welding, painting, cutting, grinding and heavy materials handling, Japanese companies have found that workers learn to live with robots and even come to appreciate their value. What's more, if workers are retained as "masters of robots," they often take great pride in the "steel-collar workers" now working for them. According to a survey by Nikkei Mechanical, about two-thirds of the Japanese companies which have installed robots use line workers to teach and maintain them.

The production floor must be ready for robotics. The most skillful users of robots in Japan today, such as Nissan, Toyota and Hitachi, were the productivity improvement champions of the '70s. They already had disciplined production floors and standardized work procedures. There is no point in introducing robots unless you can answer yes to each of these questions:

Are workers closely observing standard work procedures? Are the right materials delivered to the right place at the right time? Are quality control standards applied to all components and procedures, including accuracy and tolerance in component size? Are production machinery, jigs and tools maintained properly? Do workers properly operate stand-alone machine centers, transfer presses and the like? Robots are only as effective as their working environment.

The right robot must be chosen. Many companies are disappointed because they install robots that are "overqualified" for their tasks. On today's production floors, there are still many work stations requiring rather simple motions. There's no need for a fancy multi-directional robot to perform, say, simple loading and unloading operations.

Finally, retraining displaced blue-collars is important to successful incorporation of robots. Most companies in Japan convert displaced workers to maintenance personnel. (More ambitious companies, like Hitachi, are converting them to computer programmers!) If management pays careful attention to employees' career paths, job enrichment and assurance and offers comprehensive retraining programs, blue-collar workers learn to live with the steel-collars, and eventually a peaceful man-machine interface is established. This is too important a process for top management to leave to the shop floor or production engineering specialists.

Robots may bring a whole new perspective to both the human and strategic factors of management. They represent a brave and exciting new world, it we manage it right.

Mr. Ohmae, a director of McKinsey & Co., manages the consulting firm's offices in Tokyo and Osaka.

Improving Quality: Lessons From Hewlett-Packard

By John A. Young

I'm sure most business managers believe that their companies already produce high-quality products. We have always stressed product quality at Hewlett-Packard Co., and we have always believed—until recently—that the "find it and fix it" method of ensuring good quality was adequate and cost-effective.

But customers in recent years have come to expect much higher quality than ever before. Recognizing this, we decided several years ago to analyze in detail our methods and the costs of achieving good product quality. To our surprise, we calculated that as much as 25% of our manufacturing assets were actually tied up in *reacting to quality problems*. Using assets in this way, of course, drives up production costs and product prices, making us less competitive, in a relative sense, than we could be.

Were we, then, doing a good job of producing quality products at a fair price? And if we weren't, were other American businesses doing any better? Was it any wonder that U.S. industry was having its problems?

As we thought about this problem, it became apparent that we were facing an intriguing management challenge. With above-average quality standards already well established at Hewlett-Packard, it would be difficult to ask for better results. Yet it was apparent that major improvement was needed for us to retain a leadership position in the long run. Clearly, a bold approach was needed to convince people that a problem existed and to fully engage the entire organization in solving it.

The proper place to start, we concluded, was with a startling goal—one that would get attention. The goal we chose was a tenfold reduction in the failure rates of our products during the 1980s. We knew this represented a difficult challenge. But we also suspected that anything less dramatic wouldn't convey the importance we attached to this issue. By establishing a far-reaching goal and getting people to feel in their guts that the goal was reasonable, we felt some serious movement would begin to occur. We also knew the close linkage between higher quality, lower cost and increased productivity would lead to other beneficial results for the company.

With the goal firmly established, the second step was to identify a nucleus of leading-edge people in our organization to champion the quality cause. But to do that, we had to find ways of showing them what was possible in the quest for improved quality.

We decided to send a dozen first-line and second-line managers from manufacturing, product assurance and related fields on a fact-finding tour of Japan to see what kinds of approaches worked well there—an interesting reversal from a few short years earlier.

Not surprisingly, our study team returned with tales of impressive quality achievements and low-cost manufacturing—always in combination. What's more, they described the Japanese quality-assurance technique in remarkably simple terms: "Doing it right the first time." More than any other experience, this visit confirmed our feelings that quality improvements weren't only possible but perhaps essential to driving down prices, increasing productivity and maintaining our long-term competitiveness. And it triggered an almost crusade-like motivation among members of our study team to project this message companywide.

The next challenge was to find ways to spread the genuine enthusiasm and insight of these people throughout the organization. Several methods were available for this, and we used them all: training classes, newsletters, informal discussions and so on. But the one that seemed to have the greatest impact was peer competition—one of the strongest motivational forces available to any organization.

It was interesting to watch this type of competition take effect. People who long had thought they were doing a good job began to question long-accepted practices. Quality and productivity became the leading topics of many a coffee-break conversation, and in time more than 1,000 quality teams sprang up around the company.

When W. Edwards Deming and J. M. Juran, noted authorities on quality who helped rebuild Japanese industry following World War II, came to lecture at Hewlett-Packard, they drew packed audiences. Reports of even minor quality or productivity gains spread quickly throughout the company, inspiring others to emulate and perhaps exceed the original achievement. In time, the original nucleus of people had convinced just about everybody that much higher quality wasn't only attainable but would actually drive down costs because of productivity gains associated with doing things right the first time.

As we monitored the progress of this program, it became obvious to us that timely access to information is indispensable. Managers and supervisors who could easily call up on a computer terminal the latest parts-failure data, process schedules, rework information and so on could study cause-and-effect relationships much more clearly and make consistently better business decisions.

The logical fourth step, then, was to accelerate the spread of information-management tools throughout the company. Our intention, simply stated, was to ensure that a broad range of people were given an opportunity to access needed information, experiment with it and get instant feedback on their decisions. Perhaps more than any other factor, this process has greatly increased our knowledge of our business and made a major contribution to our overall approach to the quality/productivity issue.

What kinds of tangible results have we seen in the past few years? At one Hewlett-Packard product division, the cost of service and repair of desk-top computers was reduced 35% through improved design and manufacturing techniques. At another division, production time for two of our most popular oscilloscopes dropped 30% and product defects declined substantially, allowing us to cut prices 16%.

Vendors have been asked to become part of the total quality solution. As a result of workshops, performance evaluations and clearly stated quality specifications, there have been major improvements in the quality of parts we purchase from outside suppliers. In one case, a supplier of logic chips for our HP 3000 business computer achieved a tenfold reduction in chip-failure rates in just 15 months—to the point that we are no longer required to inspect every part that comes in.

In addition, the quality drive has helped us cut inventory companywide from 20.2% of sales at the end of fiscal 1979 to 15.5% at the end of 1982. Based on 1982 sales of $4.2 billion, that 4.7% decrease represents nearly $200 million we don't have tied up in inventory.

By our best estimates, we are perhaps a third of the way to our 10-year goal of a tenfold reduction in product-failure rates. We haven't seen any flagging in the eagerness with which our people are addressing this issue, and they continue to find new areas ripe for improvement. It may take a few more years before we know that the goal is fully within grasp, but the results to date already have made the effort well worthwhile.

Mr. Young is president and chief executive officer of Hewlett-Packard Co. He was President Reagan's chairman of the Commission on Industrial Competitiveness.

Streamlining the Factory With Just-in-Time Production

By Richard J. Schonberger

The just-in-time (JIT) production system may be the most important productivity-enhancing management innovation since Frederick Winslow Taylor's time-and-motion studies at the turn of the century. It is a Japanese innovation, and key features were perfected by Toyota. But there is nothing uniquely Japanese about JIT production. It is usable anywhere.

JIT production means producing and buying in very small quantities just in time for use. It is a simple, hand-to-mouth mode of industrial operations that directly cuts inventories and also reduces the need for storage space, racks, conveyors, forklifts, computer terminals for inventory control and material support personnel. More important, the absence of extra inventories creates an imperative to run an error-free operation because there is no cushion of excess parts to keep production going when problems crop up. Causes of errors are rooted out, never to occur again.

In some ways, JIT production is nothing new. High-volume continuous producers—for example, steel, chemical and paper companies—employ it routinely. To do otherwise would bury them in inventory. Long-term predictability of materials needed makes it possible for continuous processors to arrange for materials to flow into and through their plants steadily without inventory buildups. The Anheuser-Busch brewery in St. Louis unloads a nearly continuous stream of trucks bringing in empty cans and uses them soon enough that, on the average, there is only a two-hour supply of unfilled cans on hand.

But cans of Budweiser don't come in many different models. In most of the rest of industry, plants produce an ever-changing variety of goods, and production scheduling is complicated and irregular. JIT streamlines and simplifies the stop-and-go production of most plant operations so that they resemble continuous processing. In so doing, it forces planners and analysts to get out of their offices and get out on the floor solving real problems.

The transformation begins with inventory removal. Fewer materials are bought, and parts and products are made in smaller quantities; so-called lot-size inventories thereby shrink. Buffer stocks or safety stocks—"just-in-case" inventory—are also deliberately cut.

The immediate result is work stoppages. Plenty of them. Production comes to a standstill because feeder processes break down or produce too many defectives—and now there is no buffer stock to keep things going. This is exactly what is supposed to happen. For now the analysts and engineers pour out of their offices and mingle with foremen and workers trying to get production going again. Now the causes—bad raw materials, machine breakdown, poor training, tolerances that exceed process capabilities—get attention so that the problem may never recur.

When one round of problems is solved, inventories are cut again so that more problems crop up and get solved. Each round of problem exposure and solution increases productivity—and quality, too. In Japan extensive quality control measures blend nicely with just-in-time production because many of the problems uncovered by inventory removal are quality problems.

Some people who have studied the just-in-time system conclude that it is suitable for high-volume producers but not for smaller-volume "job shops." But many companies that call themselves job shops have some semblance of a product line; those companies can become more productive by producing in smaller lots as continuously as possible. If they don't, chances are that a Japanese competitor will emerge and capture enough market share to become a high-volume repetitive producer jeopardizing the position of the stop-and-go producers; this is what is happening to Harley-Davidson, International Harvester and Hyster.

How can Western manufacturers become JIT producers? One way is "cold turkey": Remove inventories from the shop floor, dismantle distance-spanning conveyors, move machines close together and permanently reallocate floor space that once held inventory. Spasms of work stoppages for lack of parts will soon get everyone involved in solving underlying problems.

Most companies will want to take a more incremental approach. One way is to cut the cost of machine setup, a major reason why companies make parts in large batches. Setup times can be cut by simplifying dies, machine controls, fixtures and so forth. The term "quick die change" has been in the vocabulary of American production engineers for years. But American management only heard of it recently as stories have trickled in from Japan about "single setup," which means a single-digit number of minutes, and "one-touch setup," which means zero setup (only load and unload) time.

The Kawasaki plant in Lincoln, Neb., uses another experimental approach. Occasionally it will deliberately draw down buffer stocks to near zero. The kinds of problems exposed will be recorded and assigned as improvement projects. Stocks will be allowed to build back up, and the improvement projects will proceed. As underlying problems are solved, stocks will then be permanently cut and storage floor space reallocated.

Geography is the big obstacle to just-in-time deliveries of purchased parts. When your supplier is across the country, the economies of full truck and rail car shipments often dictate infrequent large-lot buying. The Japanese companies that have opened subsidiary plants in North America—Sony, Honda, Nissan, Sanyo, Kawasaki, etc.—deal with this hurdle by resolutely seeking nearby suppliers.

Establishing those arrangements may take years of effort. In the meantime, consolidated loads from clusters of remote suppliers may permit a load to be delivered every day. Common carriers may be rejected in favor of contract shippers or company trucks, so that the day and maybe the hour of delivery may be strictly scheduled. And manufacturers must not tolerate the standard practice among U.S. suppliers of delivering plus or minus 10% of the agreed-upon purchase quantity. With no excess inventory, nor space to store it, the just-in-time company must insist on deliveries in exact quantities.

It is clear that geography is a deterrent, though not an intractable one. Aside from that, there are few obstacles. More money is not needed. The just-in-time approach features getting by with less of most of the costly resources that American manufacturers protectively surrounded themselves with in the days when capital was plentiful and interest rates were low.

The only significant obstacles to JIT are those that stand in the way of any major change in management system: reorienting people's thinking. Much of that task has been done. Just-in-time programs have been established at General Electric, the big-three auto makers, Goodyear, ROLM and various other American industrial companies.

Transforming our coughing, sputtering plants into streamlined just-in-time producers sounds like a 10- or 20-year project. It may not take that long because the innovating has been done for us. Taylor's innovation, scientific management, was readily exportable and implementable in Europe and Japan (and today the Japanese out-Taylor us all). The Japanese innovation, just-in-time, is equally transportable.

Mr. Schonberger, professor of management at the University of Nebraska, is author of "Japanese Manufacturing Techniques: Nine Hidden Lessons in Simplicity" (Free Press).

Product Diversity at Lower Cost: The Payoff From Flexible Manufacturing

By Thomas M. Hout and George Stalk Jr.

A revolution in manufacturing is completely transforming the economics of production. It is doing so by reducing the cost penalty of product diversity. The change is shaking up the rules of competition in industries ranging from automobiles to earthmoving equipment to housewares. Within companies, the traditional conflict between marketing, which wants to offer customers more models, and the factory, which has wanted to limit product line variety for the sake of production efficiency, is becoming a thing of the past.

A broad product line services a wider range of customers, but it inherently costs more than a narrow, high-volume per-model line. More models mean more machine setups, hence more downtime. Work-in-process (WIP) inventories have to increase to keep assembly areas supplied to produce a changing mix of final products and to avoid even more costly setups from low-volume lots. Also, the more diverse the product mix, the longer any given volume takes to get through a plant and the more scheduling and handling overhead it requires.

Today, however, the cost penalty for diversity is being sharply cut, thanks to a dramatic shortening of setup times in the factory. All plant operations—machining, welding, assembling and so forth—require equipment setups. Setups that used to take hours can now take minutes as a result of new, sophisticated machine tools and microprocessor control and sensory technologies. With the aid of computer controls, machines can now switch rapidly from one pre-set tool-and-die configuration to another, without the need for trips to the toolroom or the trial runs and adjustments usually necessary after manual handling. The faster setups are the key to collapsing the structure of downtime, inventory and overhead cost that plagues the conventional factory.

Toyota pioneered these developments in the 1970s, largely to avoid the cost penalties it began to see as it doubled its model range. But there is nothing uniquely Japanese about radically cutting setup time. Global competitors on both sides of the Pacific—such as Komatsu and Caterpillar in construction equipment and Matsushita and General Electric in home appliances—are adopting essentially the same practices.

One large engine manufacturer, over a five year period, roughly tripled its number of models while reducing WIP inventory by half, doubled the output per factory worker and cut material waste and rework by 40%. Across a broad range of products, reducing factory cost added after purchased materials by 15% to 35% from earlier levels is well within reach.

The marketing and competitive implications of these new plant economics are powerful. Because product variety costs less now, there will be more of it. Truck builders, for example, will pay less for the unusual engine their customers often want. Before, more product variety tended to increase finished goods inventories, causing carrying costs to rise. Now, however, shorter setups increase effective plant capacity and reduce the cycle time it takes for the complete model mix to move through the factory. This allows the manufacturers to increase their model range in finished goods stock and keep their delivery lead time constant without raising their inventory costs. Black-and-white television sets are a case in point. The model variety has risen, while prices have continued to fall.

A manufacturer may find other uses for his WIP inventory savings. He could, for instance, use them by placing more finished goods inventories at more field stocking points to widen his market presence. This is exactly how Toyota gained U.S. market share in forklift trucks in the 1970s. Toyota was the last to run out of stock in cyclical expansions.

The economies of scale which larger competitors in broadline businesses have enjoyed are changing. The new setup economics will tend to reduce the cost benefits of size between two competitors with similar product mix. Traditionally, plant scale economies have been of two kinds—plant-wide savings from greater automation and fixed overheads spread over more volume, and the benefits of more dedicated machines and assembly lines that never need setups. Shorter setups will have little effect on the first advantage but will significantly dilute the second. Full-line producers with smaller market shares may suffer less manufacturing disadvantage than before.

As with any change in the rules, the competitor who exploits more swiftly and completely will gain the advantage. Industry leaders typically have greater engineering resources and more opportunities for high-markup, low-volume specialty products which shorter setups would favor. (General Motors over Ford in cars and Du Pont over Monsanto in synthetic fibers are examples.) But industry leaders may resist change. Engineering and production managers, for instance, may be heavily committed to their current systems. But the new setup economics is a powerful lever, and it's unlikely that a leader will be able to hold its lead without making these new investments.

This set of economic relationships is fairly straightforward, but making it work for you is not. It requires both capital and imagination—typically a doubling or tripling of equipment investment and a thorough rethinking of plant flows, layout and line-balancing logic. The role of workers is also important. Greater flexibility and intelligence are demanded of both people and machines. Machine tools and material handling devices must be redesigned. Experimentation is necessary: Radical systems that work take time to develop.

Developing the actual working system will most likely demand some proprietary engineering advances. Off-the-shelf technology will go only so far. Unusual savings will often come only from an original, unique machine-tool configuration or a component redesigned to accommodate automatic handling. Companies whose cultures have devalued manufacturing will have trouble.

In addition, component suppliers have to make comparable changes in production operations if their deliveries are to match the manufacturer's shorter runs, lower inventories and greater variety. More frequent and rigorously scheduled deliveries are critical. Usually the manufacturer must educate the supplier, specify a tighter set of dimensional tolerances and may even help underwrite his investment. In general, more supplier coordination and discipline are needed.

The payoffs from these investments, however, can be enormous. First, shorter setup time increases the use of machines and direct labor. It also reduces foreman and indirect labor time spent during setup. Second, shorter setups lower work-in-process inventory. They cut down on stock orders and the buffer inventory one needs ahead of and behind any operation. Third, simplifying traditionally long and complex setups reduces maintenance costs, raises production yields and cuts down time spent solving problems. It's usually the difficulty, not the frequency, of setups that causes broken tools, high machine wear and work rejected for being out-of-tolerance.

Reducing setup times by a factor of five or 10—quite common now for able manufacturers—dramatically increases the effective capacity of machines and plants. Each unit of output spends less time in the factory, reducing normal burden rates. Lower inventories eliminate not only their carrying costs but also the number of material handlers and schedulers who manage them. Inventory turns go up by multiples, not mere percentages. Higher yields and lower maintenance reduce the cost per usable unit of output. The higher effective capacity allows slower machine running speeds with no loss of output, thus improving product quality by reducing machine wear.

Once the heavy investment is made by one competitor, the high interest rates associated with inventory carrying costs and uncertain, shifting demand patterns will differentiate him from the competitor who did not invest. Both will want to reduce inventories and change product mix quickly. The producer with a short setup time can achieve these without cost penalty; the other cannot. The latter can increase inventory turns via more setups only at the expense of more machine downtime and considerably more indirect labor time spent in setup.

The strategic payoff from the investment lies in marketing, and in better control of competitors. Shorter setup times enable a company to serve distribution channels better and to capture, at acceptable cost, higher-price, low-volume products. Broad-line producers everywhere will have to reckon with these new economics of diversity.

Mr. Hout is a Chicago-based vice president of the Boston Consulting Group. Mr. Stalk is a principal in the consulting firm's Tokyo office.

To Exploit New Technology, Know When to Junk the Old

By Richard N. Foster

Everyone knows the sad tales of companies that seemingly did everything right, yet lost competitive leadership as a result of technological change. Du Pont was beaten by Celanese when bias-ply tire cords changed from nylon to polyester. B.F. Goodrich was beaten by Michelin when the radial overtook the bias-ply tire. NCR wrote off $139 million in electromechanical inventory, and the equipment to make it, when solid-state point-of-sale terminals entered the market. Indeed, none of the leading vacuum tube manufacturers in 1957 remained as a competitive force by 1977.

These companies lost even though they were low-cost producers. They lost even though they were close to their customers. They lost even though they were market-share leaders. They lost because they failed to make an effective transition from old to new technology.

These judgments, of course, are easy to make in hindsight. It's much more difficult to predict today what technologies will dominate the marketplace five or 10 years from now. Even so, there are some companies—for example IBM, AT&T, Hewlett-Packard, Dow and Eli Lilly—which over the years have persistently stayed at the forefront of technical change in their industries. They may not bat 1.000, but their average has generally been over .300, enough to put them in the top ranks. And they owe their relative success to a recognition of five realities of technically based economic competition.

First, they recognize that all products and processes have performance limits, and that the closer one comes to these limits the more expensive it becomes to squeeze out the next generation of performance improvements. The technological winners therefore do systematic basic research to understand the limits of each technology, and when they see that the limits of an existing technology are being approached, they realize that greater opportunities may lie in a completely different one.

The classic example of this kind of analysis occurred when Bell Labs recognized that electromechanical switches could never be made small enough to produce really compact machines. Mervin Kelly, then director of research at Bell, felt that a way around the limits might be found in quantum mechanics and formed the team that invented the transistor. A more recent example was IBM's effort, through its Watson Research Labs, to discover the practical limits on computer chip density. This analysis of limits had a major impact on the 43xx and 308x computer series.

Second, companies that stay ahead technologically take all competition seriously. Normal competitor analyses seem to implicitly assume that the most serious competitors will be the ones with the largest resources. In technological competition this is frequently not the case. Texas Instruments was a $5 million to $10 million company in 1955 when it took on the mighty vacuum tube manufacturers—RCA, General Electric, Sylvania and Westinghouse—and beat all of them with its semiconductor technology. Boeing was nearly bankrupt when it successfully introduced the commercial jet plane, vanquishing the larger and more financially secure Lockheed, McDonnell and Douglas Corps.

Third, if there is substantial technical potential in a new technology, you have to attack to win or even play in the game. Attacking means gaining access to the new technology, training people on its use, investing in capacity to use

65

it, devising strategies to protect your position and holding off on investments in mature lines.

Most companies have a big problem with this approach, arguing that they need to recoup their prior capital investment in the old technology. But this argument implicitly assumes that the customer will continue to buy the old product even if it is less economic. This rarely happens. The logic is false. The returns will not be made in any case. Du Pont learned this when it continued to invest in nylon tire cords, only to be beaten by the smaller Celanese, which was investing in the newer polyester cords. Lever learned it in the detergent business when it was beaten by Procter & Gamble, which introduced the first synthetic detergent. Certainly it is wiser to invest in assets that will make money rather than reinvest in assets that will not make money.

Fourth, the attack has to begin early. The substitution of one product or process for another proceeds at a slow pace and then explodes—rarely in a predictable fashion. One cannot wait for the explosion to occur to react. There is simply not enough time. B.F. Goodrich lost 60 percentage points of market share to Michelin in four years. Texas Instruments passed RCA in sales of active electronic devices in five to six years.

Moreover, one cannot rely on economic measures of performance for an early warning. Frequently the market in which the technological switch is taking place is growing, and the growth covers up the decay, until it becomes catastrophic. Tracking of the relative technical performance of the old and new approaches, always mindful of the limits of each, is perhaps the best early warning indicator one can get.

Bell Labs recognized this when it saw the need to switch from germanium transistors to silicon transistors in the 1950s. International oil companies are beginning to recognize the need to measure technological progress as well as economic performance. Electronic hardware manufacturers are observing that it is getting increasingly expensive to produce the next generation of performance improvements, for example in moving from the 64K random-access memory to the 256K. Thus we may see a slowdown in the rate of introduction of "new" RAMs in the next five years and increases in other areas of technology—for example, software packages which use the RAMs.

Fifth, a close tie is needed between the CEO and the chief technical officer to accomplish the necessary changes. Without this, the leadership needed to translate ever-changing business needs into technical programs and to adjust business strategies to respond to changing technological possibilities will be missing. William Baker, former president of Bell Labs, had this relationship with several chairmen at AT&T; Ralph Gomory, director of research, and Louis Branscomb, chairman of the corporate technical committee, have it at IBM. Malcolm Pruitt, formerly director of R&D, had it at Dow. But, according to the Conference Board, these relationships are the exceptions. In the U.S. today only one CEO in five considers his top technical officer a part of the inner circle.

The U.S. is atop an exploding knowledge base. We are well positioned to regain our lost international competitiveness if we are clever about our management of technology. Learning the lessons of the winners is an important first step.

Mr. Foster, a director in the New York office of McKinsey & Co., heads the consulting firm's work on technology management.

What Quality Circles Can and Cannot Do

By Kenichi Ohmae

Quality control circles, so spectacularly successful in Japan in recent years, hold little promise of short-term gains. They take generations to bear fruit, and cannot be expected to succeed if they are ordered by edict. Moreover, the scope of their achievement, though impressive over time, is limited.

A QC circle is a group of about 10 relatively autonomous workers from the same division of a company who volunteer to meet for an hour or so once or twice a month. After work (usually they are paid overtime), they discuss ways to improve the quality of their products, the production process in their part of the plant and the working environment. Their long-term objective is to build a sense of responsibility for improving quality, but the immediate goal is to exchange ideas in a place uninhibited by barriers of age, sex or company rank.

Japan's experience has revealed several preconditions for the success of QC circles. Some may be indigenous.

First, the work force must be intelligent and reasonably well-educated. Members of the circles must be able to use statistical and industrial engineering analysis. They must know what it takes to make things work on a nuts and bolts level, and they must be able to brainstorm together. It is no coincidence that the Japanese companies which have been most successful with these circles and other participatory methods for improving productivity (Hitachi, Teijin, Asahi Glass and Nippon Kokan) are also well-known for their fine recruiting and internal training programs.

Second, management must be willing to trust workers with cost data and important information, and to give them the authority to implement their ideas. At Japanese companies with successful QC programs, managers have tended to work their way up through the ranks: They really believe in their work force. It is no surprise to them that groups of workers, if given information and authority to experiment by trial and error, will be able to reduce downtime, waste or reworking—the sorts of questions that the circles are most effective in addressing.

Third, workers must be willing and eager to cooperate with each other. Unlike the suggestion box and other worker incentive programs which reward individuals, QC programs reward groups. A genuine "team spirit" is therefore necessary: Workers must be willing to express themselves and find fulfillment by reaching agreement.

Moreover, if authority in production decisions is to be decentralized down to the level of these circles, then the circles have to be able to cooperate with each other lest they work at cross-purposes. Unless there is a spirit of cooperation within the work force, an attitude that talking a problem through with peers is more rewarding than taking it up to management, a company is better off using individual carrots instead of the circles. Otherwise, it may find night shifts undoing the improvements of day shifts.

One of the most important features of QC circles in Japan is that they did not originate with senior management. They spring rather from a voluntary, grass-roots movement of workers and middle managers from across the nation.

The spearhead has been the Union of Japanese Scientists and Engineers, or Nikka-Giren. In 1962, it began publishing a magazine, later named FQC, which called for quality control circles among factory workers and foremen and helped precipitate a change from the Western concept of quality control as the prerogative of technical experts. The magazine circulated widely among industrial workers, who bought it themselves (it cost them about the same as a pack of cigarets) rather than receiving it through their employers, and read it together—in a circle. The magazine, together with a generation of supervisors familiar with QC concepts from the '50s, helped initiate massive training of non-supervisors.

The Nikka-Giren Union continues to have great influence. It publishes case histories of successful QC circles and sponsors regional and national conferences, where circle participants from different companies share their experiences.

Since most Japanese companies are very secretive with each other, this openness seems a paradox. But the movement was initially popular in the steel and shipbuilding industries, where there was a tradition of letting other companies freely inspect production methods and facilities. Had the movement started in the Japanese camera or auto industry, it is doubtful whether the current openness and cross-fertilization would have developed. Today, cross-fertilization is one of the keys to the success of the circles in Japan—the exchanges not only encourage but also keep workers interested in the process.

Quality control circles don't run themselves. They must be revitalized. Most important is the specific set of goals they are given and a strong manager who coordinates QCC changes with corporate objectives. In companies which use both the suggestion box and quality control circle, management can gather directly from workers ideas which may require significant capital expenditures and at the same time use suggestion box successes to encourage QCC efforts.

Management spends more time today on sustaining existing circles than starting new ones, understanding that their effects are incremental and cumulative. In 1951, Toyota received 700 proposals from its new worker participation program. Today it gets 500,000 per year, which save a reported $230 million.

But there are limits to what the circles can do. The abrupt quantum leaps in cost reduction that the Japanese have achieved in industries as diverse as steel and consumer electronics do not result from QC circles. Instead they come from major strategic decisions about new technologies and plants and entirely new ways of producing and delivering a product.

At Ricoh, for example, it wasn't a circle that figured out how to redesign the business system by changing the technology, manufacturing and marketing to completely change the game in plain paper copiers. Nor was it the circles that led to the elimination of inventory ("Kanban" system) at Toyota. QC circles, composed of workers from a single division, can't come up with these bold strokes.

Nor can they replace strategy. Indeed in many industries a single-minded focus on productivity improvements and concomitant quality control activities may be less important for success than focused R&D and targeted marketing.

Quality control circles work best when they are part of what the Japanese call total quality control, which embraces concerns about the entire spectrum of a business. And they are one of a number of productivity improvement techniques which work best when put together. As the Japanese would say, it's like collecting dust to make a mountain. But somebody has to envision the mountain, and know which way the wind is blowing.

Mr. Ohmae, a director of McKinsey & Co., runs the consulting firm's offices in Tokyo and Osaka. He is author of "The Mind of the Strategist" (McGraw-Hill).

Process Design as Important as Product Design

By John Mayo

"Japan Does Away With Quality Control." An article with this provocative title must have come as quite a shock to those impressed by Japan's traditional concern with and commitment to manufacturing quality.

Has Japan decided that quality is no longer a priority? Hardly. What it has decided is that traditional quality-control techniques are no longer sufficient, and that something beyond these traditional approaches is needed. A similar realization has taken place at certain companies in the U.S., AT&T among them.

Traditional quality-control programs in the U.S. and elsewhere have relied on a combination of inspections and statistical quality-control methods, such as control charts. The emphasis has been on tightly controlling manufacturing processes. But about 10 years ago, when many products—and their associated manufacturing processes—began to assume then-unheard-of degrees of complexity, managers and engineers were forced to redesign their approach to quality control.

The number of manufacturing steps involved in many of today's products is tremendous. For example, it is not unusual in the making of a state-of-the-art integrated circuit to have 200 manufacturing steps. As the control of these complex processes becomes an unwieldy task, the emphasis at some companies has shifted to reducing the influence that variations in manufacturing processes would have on the final products. At AT&T we have come to realize that high quality can be achieved in complex products only by starting at the front end of the product cycle, with the design of both the product and its manufacturing process.

A new and somewhat revolutionary approach to quality control has thus been developed: "design quality," or what some call "off-line" quality control. Broadly stated, off-line quality control includes all quality engineering activities carried out before a product goes into full-scale production. It is not enough to come up with a product that works well when manufactured exactly according to the design specifications; the product must also be easy to manufacture and insensitive to variability on the factory floor.

An example may help clarify how these principles can be applied. Many AT&T products contain hundreds or even thousands of circuit packs. (A circuit pack is a collection of electronic components mounted on a printed circuit board.) A critical step in circuit-pack fabrication is the mass soldering of up to several hundred components to a printed circuit board. This mass soldering process can be cumbersome to control, since the optimum soldering machine settings depend on many factors, such as the physical layout of the printed circuit board, the type of components and their orientation, and the total number of components.

Rather than continually striving to control this process, we designed a soldering technique that was much less sensitive to the variations in the manufacturing process. A new flux (a chemical that prepares the surface for soldering) was developed to increase the effectiveness of the mass soldering process without requiring a change in the soldering machine settings. The key idea is that it is cheaper to reduce the influence of manufacturing line variability than to try to control it.

The same principles can be applied to product design. For example, AT&T recently developed an integrated circuit that could be used in many products to amplify voice signals. As originally designed, the circuit had to be manufactured very precisely to avoid variations in the strength of the signal. Such a circuit would have been costly to make because of stringent quality controls needed during the manufacturing process. But our engineers, after testing and analyzing the design, realized that if the resistance of the circuit were reduced—a minor change with no associated costs—the circuit would be far less sensitive to manufacturing variations. The result was a 40% improvement in quality.

Unfortunately, many industries are still stranded in the old "inspect and fix" mode. One American laboratory I know of was testing a new product design for durability. Components that failed during the tests were simply replaced by better quality (and more expensive) counterparts. No attempt was made to redesign the product around the less expensive components. The final design released for manufacture therefore exceeded the original budgeted cost. This story is all too common in America.

The Japanese, on the other hand, have excelled in redesigning for quality, largely because, in the past, they built an economy around improving products designed elsewhere. One Japanese watchmaker found that it isn't necessary to use an expensive quartz crystal to achieve high accuracy in a wristwatch. An inexpensive capacitor could compensate for variations in a cheaper crystal without sacrificing overall accuracy.

If American industry embraces design quality it will realize not only improved products, but lower costs as well.

Mr. Mayo is executive vice president, Network Systems, at AT&T Bell Laboratories.

Don't Expect Too Much From Your Computer System

By Richard L. Van Horn

In a world appropriately filled with glowing promises for computers, managers are well advised to reflect on what computers are not. For more than 20 years, businesses ranging from banking to bookmaking have embraced computer systems with a level of hope and enthusiasm normally reserved for risk-free, high-profit investments.

In the sobering light of actual use, some firms have realized many or all of their high expectations, but others have discovered that computer systems are hardly risk-free and certainly are no guarantee of higher profits. A computer system represents an expensive, high-technology capital investment, and such investments often promise high returns only for high risk. At a minimum, such investments demand thoughtful and continuing attention from management.

A computer system, no matter how successfully applied to a problem, does not guarantee improvement. For example, a computerized inventory system with poor ordering rules will reorder the wrong quantities of the wrong parts faster and more consistently than its manual counterpart. The computer's outstanding attributes of speed, large memory, consistency and the ability to follow complex logical instructions are of value only to the extent that they are applied within a good management process. Computers are a complement to, not a substitute for, careful management.

Computer users must remember that precision is not accuracy. Without question, computers operate with great precision. They can perform long and complex processing of instruction, text and numbers without introducing any new errors. As a result, computer output neatly printed on display screen or paper is often treated like pages from Holy Writ. This computational fundamentalism is, as many managers have found through costly experience, a dangerous assumption.

Computer output can be better than the data put in, in the sense that computers can find and correct certain types of errors. But many errors in input data are impossible to detect, particularly those made at an earlier stage in collecting the information by other people or recording devices. From salesmen to machinists, people tend to "adjust" input to fit their view of the world.

All large programs contain errors, at least in the sense that they do not always work as either their authors or users intended. Because of the complexity of large business programs, that may contain thousands of instructions, errors remain even after years of use. A healthy skepticism about the accuracy of the output is the best antidote to being stung by a hidden program bug.

Some business problems are just too complex or ill-defined for computers to solve. Scheduling machines in a job-shop, for example, is a problem that is "solved" every day by people, but may need months of computing time for an exact, numeric solution—if any is possible. And each set of new or changed orders would require further month-long computer runs to take these everyday alterations into account.

In making the decision whether to market a new laundry detergent (or magazine, car or frozen food), computers can keep track of survey results, calculate costs, analyze a range of assumptions and handle other pieces of quantitative bookkeeping. But in the end, those making the decision must fall back on that strange mixture of experience and gut feeling we call human judgment. As with factory sched-uling or investments in the stock market, computers can help, but they certainly can't guarantee success.

A company overwhelmed by paper work or plagued by decision-making channels too complex for its employees to navigate certainly should consider computer support. If a software vendor has a program or set of programs that can be used essentially off-the-shelf, that computer application could be operating satisfactorily in a few weeks or months. But tailoring a new package to a reasonably complex appli-cation of any kind—order processing, inventory, accounting or market analysis—will take several years of analysis, design and testing.

In many problem areas, management should not—indeed, cannot—wait for a computer system solution. Urgent prob-lems should be attacked with better procedures, tighter con-trols, more manpower and the whole range of traditional management tools. Aside from preventing a possible operat-ing disaster, the short-term correction of problems often pro-vides valuable insight to designers of longer-term, comput-erized solutions.

Regrettably, even applying computers carefully and cor-rectly in every respect may yield little if any benefit. There is a widespread belief that "doing things right" is the key to good management. In truth, many of the activities that go on in a firm have no noticeable effect on cash flow or profit. Better—more timely, more accurate, more complete—ac-counting information may neither sell more products nor reduce costs. Peter Drucker summarized the issue aptly with his view that the critical management function is not to do things right but to do the right things.

The Japanese auto companies provide some interesting illustrations. It was the U.S. companies that developed and applied outstanding decision rules and computer systems for managing inventories of expensive components such as starters and alternators. The Japanese simply built the parts plants next door to the auto assembly plant, and got rid of inventories altogether!

In the final analysis, we must both apply computers correctly and apply them to the right problems if we want to have a significant impact on the welfare of the firm.

Mr. Van Horn, formerly head of management systems for Rand Corp., is chancellor of the University of Houston.

Taking the Bugs Out of Computer Spread Sheets

By Robert M. Freeman

If you're like most managers, the decisions you make based on personal computer spread sheets are already big and getting bigger. The scope of those decisions is getting wider. And, the likelihood for serious problems is growing.

A Dallas-based oil and gas company recently fired several executives for oversights costing millions of dollars in an acquisition deal. The errors were traced to faulty financial analysis in a spread-sheet model.

How can we avoid disasters such as the one in Dallas? What are the problems we should look out for? How can we improve spread sheets so that they will improve high-quality decision making?

The old computing dictum, "garbage in, garbage out," used to imply a clear answer to the question of spread sheets' reliability: They were just as good or bad as you made them. But the acclaim given personal computers and the wholesale adoption of spread sheets as planning tools seems to have turned the old adage on its ear. "Garbage in, garbage out" has become "garbage in, gospel out."

Managers and executives responsible for decisions based on personal computer spread sheets should look behind those reassuring printouts to the logic and makeup of the spread-sheet models themselves.

The following problems are accompanied by real examples taken from businesses I have analyzed or worked with:

1) A model is logically inconsistent; rules applied to one part of the spread sheet should be applied to another part, but are not. In forecasting revenues, a California manufacturer applied price discounts to one part of a product line, but overlooked them when forecasting sales of complementary products. Actual sales for the complementary lines turned out to be higher than forecast, and bottlenecks resulted when production could not keep up with delivery.

2) A model, though logically consistent, is conceptually flawed. Here, bad formulas are faithfully reproduced throughout a spread-sheet model. A finance officer with a large savings and loan association submitted five-year forecasts for divisional profits. However, a mistake in a formula for compound growth resulted in the figures becoming progressively overstated for years two through five of the forecast.

3) Data format is inconsistent or garbled. Typically, these problems occur when different types of data are used side by side in the same or parallel model. For example, a national retailer, accounting for manpower needs, discovered field reports stated in persons, man-hours, man-days and man-months. Consolidation proved impossible until an exhaustive rewrite of field reports was completed.

4) The wrong tool is used for the task. This problem is common and growing. An international distributor of industrial goods based its plans for sales to a South American country on an analysis of that country's manufacturing capacity. But, the distributor's products were only used in secondary manufacturing, a small part of the country's total output. The distinction was not made in the spread sheet so that sales were far below forecasts; production and inventory costs ended up consuming thousands of extra dollars.

In all of these examples, gross inconsistencies or major problems will quickly stand out. Many times, though, subtle problems will not be readily detected.

Worse, problem detection becomes more and more difficult as data users are removed from the data's source. This frequently occurs when one department uses data generated by another department's spread sheets. Even if detected, problems may be nearly impossible to trace, not to mention correct.

Managers are not without tools to address this mushrooming problem. A carefully followed set of "spread-sheet audit" procedures combined with software for isolating mistakes can all but eliminate most common spread-sheet problems.

The steps to be followed are straightforward:

1) Insist on an audit of all spread sheets used for important decision making. Recently available software, such as Docu-Calc for Apple computers or the Spreadsheet Auditor for IBM PCs, gives two-dimensional printouts with detailed listings of the spread-sheet formulas—thus making verification of the model's underpinnings routine.

This ability to examine the makeup of a spread-sheet model is the best insurance that the model is conceptually sound, logically consistent and appropriate to the decision task at hand.

2) Create and enforce an audit trail. As data, printouts or diskettes move beyond their source, this becomes indispensable. In addition to the printout of the formulas mentioned above, an audit trail should include the name of the model's author, the date it was created, a unique name or number, what type of input and output are expected, and a brief narrative describing the purpose and operation of the model.

3) Establish responsibility for the model. Do not let it wander. Changes to the model should be made by authorized personnel only. More importantly, managers using other departments' spread sheets should be responsible for them as if they were their own. Enforcement of this rule will bolster enforcement of rule No. 2 above. A manager responsible for a spread sheet's output will insist on an audit trail and will not just blindly "plug in his own numbers."

4) Require a re-audit each time the model is modified. Document these changes in the audit trail. Spread sheets seem to take on a life of their own, growing in size and

complexity as more and more variables are factored into the model. Even minor changes can have unintended effects on otherwise sound spread sheets.

In addition to these specific rules, a final suggestion may be useful: Raise the visibility of the issue. Find out who is using spread sheets for what sort of decision making. If the decisions are important, ensure that procedures similar to these are implemented and followed.

Mr. Freeman is a marketing manager at Sytek Inc., a Mountain View, Calif., firm specializing in local area networks for computer communications.

3

People
You Work With

To Raise Productivity, Try Saying Thank You

By Jack Falvey

People work for love and money. Few of us ever seem to get enough of either. There are no great behavioral science secrets to good management. If you will give top priority to supporting and paying your people you will be blessed with results beyond your dreams.

Managers often think of themselves as systems specialists or problem solvers or functional experts. They lose sight of the common sense practicality of getting others committed to doing things for them willingly. The essence of good management is letting people know what you expect, inspecting what is done, and supporting those things that are done well.

We don't even know the design limitations of a human being. All we do know is that even the most committed people seldom exceed 15% or 20% of their brain capacity in a normal day's work.

Average people can easily double or triple their output without even exerting themselves. If managers would begin thinking in terms of doing things *for* their people, instead of *to* them, we would see productivity increases off the scales.

Bob Bennett, the general manager of WCVB-TV in Boston, recently said thank you to his 300 employees for their part in making their station a Metromedia affiliate.

He gave a first-class 10-year party for everyone, presented engraved personalized Boston Rockers to those who had been there since the station's start in 1972, and then, a couple of weeks later without anyone getting wind of it, divided up three-quarters of a million dollars as a bonus to all employees. Most received a check for $2,250.

As you might imagine, Channel 5 has never had any difficulty in attracting top talent and technical people.

At Mary Kay Cosmetics the budget for this year's legendary Dallas-based sales seminar and awards meeting was $2.5 million, and the attendees all paid their own expenses. If you are successful with Mary Kay you earn it, but when you do earn it everyone sure will know it when they see your pink Cadillac. Mary Kay Ash has built a major corporation by recognizing the contributions of her employees. She doesn't solve problems, she just says thank you as often as she can, and in some of the most creative ways imaginable.

These managers don't have Santa Claus complexes. They are leaders in their highly competitive fields because they invest in their people.

These are big and spectacular examples, but little companies can do little things that carry returns out of all proportion to costs. Dan Daly, the owner of Daly & Co., an executive search and placement business with only 30 employees, extended medical benefits for three months to one of his people who had left the company to relocate to Europe and needed interim coverage. That support message said that Dan cares about his people and will treat them as best he can. What kind of commitment do you think he gets from his group? They have made him number one in his market area.

Don Rasmussen of Wang Laboratories just finished running the annual kickoff meeting for his Minneapolis District. All of the administrative and support personnel attended the resort-based three-day work and awards gathering. When it came time to give out recognition for last year's results, some of the credit and order-processing people carried off some of the biggest plaques. The behind-the-scenes support personnel received some of the longest and loudest standing ovations.

Again and again, the things that industry leaders do in this area are identical.

From NCR's 100% Club starting in the early 1900s to IBM's letters of commendation for just about everything, saying thank you and recognizing positive contributions have always been characteristic of long-term success.

Here are a few things you can do right now with no increase in budget, but with big returns.

Make a list of everyone who works for you. Before the week is out tell each one personally what he has contributed this week and how much you appreciate his efforts.

Criticism is to be avoided at all costs (there is no such thing as constructive criticism, all criticism is destructive). If you must correct someone, never do it after the fact. Bite your tongue and hold off until he is about to do the same thing again and then challenge him to make a more positive contribution. If you can do that consistently, you will be earning your pay as a professional manager.

Set up informal visits with your people. Listen and use your eyes to pick up on what is going on. Don't look for problems, look for strengths and things done well. Make something out of every positive thing you can find. As a manager, your words and actions carry impact much greater than you expect. Just a small effort with these techniques will have almost immediate effect. A concentrated, disciplined, and sustained thrust in these directions will produce incredible returns.

Publish everything positive you can find. Print is cheap. Its rewards are long-lasting.

Put positive notes on everything and send them back to everyone.

Eliminate performance reviews. No matter how good you may be at them, and few managers are, they always have a negative impact. There is no need for formal reviews if you give informal ones constantly.

Fred Stephens at Gillette was required to give a six-month evaluation to a new employee. He did it after four months by means of a handwritten note to the executive's wife telling her how much he appreciated the work her husband was doing.

That little technique didn't come out of the corporate policy manual. It did show that even in a highly structured environment a little positive innovation is possible.

How innovative can you be? Do you realize the impact you have on others? Can you reduce or eliminate the negatives in your dealings with your people? Will you do the searching and analysis necessary to uncover positive contributions? Can you name the strengths of all of your people? Can you say something complimentary to everyone by the end of this week?

As simple and as straightforward as all this is, it is really a tremendously difficult professional challenge. Just how good are you as a professional manager? If results are produced by committed people, just how much love and money can you spread around to build that commitment and those results? Go do something nice for someone right now.

Mr. Falvey runs a consulting company, Intermark, in Londonderry, N.H.

Every Worker a Manager: Shunning Bureaucracy at People Express

By Donald Burr

I work in one of the most regulated, bureaucratic industries in the world. Yet I have worked hard at my company to dispel the notion that one must develop a bureaucracy to deal with other bureaucracies. We at People Express believe that our company has remained competitive because of a tenacious commitment to strong growth without the development of a bureaucratic infrastructure.

In this industry, as in most, 99% of everything competitors do is the same. But there's that whisker of difference in style that often makes the difference between success or failure. Most major airlines have bureaucratic support structures, which they credit as responsible for their competitive edge. At People Express we put our money on the flexibility that comes from operating as a nonbureaucratic, entrepreneurial organization.

I can't say that our creative powers are so strong and vibrant that we always whip the other guys. Sometimes bureaucratic smoothness is more important than creative flair. In Denver and Orlando, People Express was able to beat out the competition for the best gates in the airports because the critical edge in those contests was speed and flexibility, which our organization has. On the other hand, we were beat out in San Francisco and Chicago because the other airlines could throw their bureaucratic weight behind the effort to win.

One of the greatest dangers facing a company trying to avoid the development of an internal bureaucracy is the formation of staff niches—positions that require no direct contact with customers. There are folks at People Express who would love to get into an office, put their feet up on a desk and be in charge of our relationship with the Federal Aviation Administration. Perhaps regulatory bureaucrats have become enormously powerful because of the amount of attention they have been given by corporate bureaucrats.

If, however, you tell people they are valued primarily by the way they exercise their leadership around the customer, then their creative energies are focused on the customer rather than the bureaucrat. And the concept of constant interacting with customers cannot be restricted to one level of management. Every level below me, including all the officers, must spend time working directly with the customers. The next time you fly People Express, your coffee may be served by People's chief financial officer, Bob McAdoo, who is a certified flight attendant and flies weekly.

Every worker at People Express is a manager. There is no classification of an individual who is not a manager. Customer-service managers, maintenance managers, flight managers, general managers and managing officers—there's nothing else. No one has a secretary at People Express. We run a company that this year will do about $600 million in volume without having one secretary. I answer my own phone and I hand write my own letters. Needless to say, I don't write much.

Our managers' daily assignments change regularly here. Customer-service managers (CSMs) will on one day be responsible for counter "M" and on another day will be responsible for organizing the recruiting of 50 people. But those responsible for the results in well-designated performance areas are always known. We have 20 CSMs or maintenance managers working with one team manager. That team manager has a direct relationship with a general manager, who has a direct relationship to one of our five managing officers. Every person at People Express is no more than three steps away from me or from a managing officer. So when something goes wrong, I always know where to go to find the person responsible.

Because all of our workers perform both customer-related services and classic bureaucratic chores, over a period of time this leads to many differences of perspectives in dealing with an issue, which leads to greater creativity, which leads to greater innovation. We have many flight managers (pilots) who couldn't even spell "facilities" when they arrived here. Now, they are conversant with folks who spend most of their time dealing with facility issues: How do you get them, how do you construct them, how do you make them work right? This gives us a richer work force.

Ironically, this policy has improved our relations with government bureaucracies. Rather than assign corporate bureaucrats to deal with regulators, our own flight managers become directly involved in that task. The people who can say, "I know that this begins to happen when I bank a 727," deal with the regulators and help write the manuals. Therefore, the relationship with FAA inspectors who actually go out there and fly is better because they talk the same language.

The biggest complaints I get from those who work here are that they want more pay and that they have trouble with their work lives. Both stock ownership (every new worker purchases 100 shares of People Express upon entry) and profit sharing (a third of all profits generated goes to the managers, a third to People Express and a third to stockholders) go a long way toward addressing the first problem. We have an enormous investment in our managers, and they have an enormous investment in People Express.

But, of course, no one is ever satisfied with the amount of money he or she is getting, so that issue doesn't concern me as much as the work-life issue. We're trying to create an environment in which people care about what they're doing because it's relevant to them. So when managers say they have a problem with their work lives, we listen intently. It strikes at the heart of a system in which everyone is a manager. For example, with regard to scheduling, we have broken down managers into operating groups of 250 people. Each group has a specified amount of work to do and comes up with its own arrangement of how it plans to carry out that work. In that way, our managers feel much more in control.

When you're trying to maintain the honesty of face-to-face discussions such as these, the introduction of third-party negotiators is virtually unthinkable. People who are afraid to do their own negotiating are the ones most receptive to unions, and those are not the people we look for here. We've gone to great lengths to avoid a unionized presence here because our competitive strategy depends upon free individuals doing what they freely enjoy; bureaucratic unions telling their members as a bloc when, what and how much they can do runs counter to that style.

What we are now doing at People Express is developing the base upon which long-term profitability can be built. And such a base must begin with people who trust and have faith in the organization. Our steadfast opposition to the development of bureaucratic middle layers is an integral part of this strategy. Once an organization begins to protect and coddle all those people who have got themselves into the cushy little foot-on-the-desk bureaucratic jobs, the organization has lost its creative edge. Protection of this bureaucratic elite becomes more important than providing the best service for the customer. That's exactly what happens in most corporations. But it's not going to happen here at People Express.

Mr. Burr is founder and chairman of People Express.

Sobering Advice on Office Alcoholics

By Nicholas A. Pace, M.D.

There is no better time of year than the festive, holiday season to reflect on one of the most difficult personnel problems confronting managers: coping with an alcoholic executive. Of course, managers must be careful to distinguish between alcoholics and those who merely get a bit carried away at the office party.

There is a difference between social drinkers and alcoholics. Some generalities can be made here: If you have to drink to be social, it's not social drinking; a social drinker can have one or two and go home, without being dragged away from that "last drink." Generally, alcoholism is based not on how much a person drinks, but on a person's physical, behavioral and metabolic reaction to alcohol. If alcohol interferes with an individual's health, work or personal life, then that individual has a problem with alcohol.

Understandably, the work situation can deteriorate rapidly if the alcoholic executive is in constant contact with clients, or if his or her decisions are strategically critical to the company. And by the time the manager can spot signs of alcoholism at work, it is already a problem at home. The alcoholic will tell you his domestic problems have created drinking problems, rather than the other way around.

If the alcoholic is deemed too important to lose, or if the

company feels a moral obligation to give the executive every chance to get back on the track, then the manager in charge of dealing with the problem executive must work in very deliberate ways.

A big mistake can be made if you approach the alcoholic without knowing what you are doing. The first thing a manager should do is sit down with a professional who understands the disease of alcoholism (not all doctors and counselors do). The biggest mistakes I have seen were created when managers suddenly realized they were in over their heads and were moving toward a personal confrontation they were not prepared to deal with. As with any management decision, know where you are going with your plan.

Before confronting the executive with an alcohol problem, be sure you have a thorough case. Don't make a diagnosis because a person has slurred speech or alcohol on his or her breath—but it should be noted. Make a record of tardiness, absenteeism, errors and complaints from others. However, be aware that if the alcoholic executive can, he will delegate increasingly, and it becomes harder to afix responsibility for particular actions. If this makes verification difficult, have the executive's boss give the person an unexpected assignment in the afternoon and check the performance.

Expect roadblocks. The most powerful of these is the executive's secret weapon: the secretary. The secretary realizes, perhaps without being conscious of the executive's problem, that her boss is "no good" after lunch, so she does not schedule much in the afternoon. She says he is in conference when he is not.

When you have enough documentation over a specified period, then carefully stage a confrontation by the ranking supervisor—department head, president, chairman, or whoever ranks above the problem executive. At the meeting, do not be punitive or moralistic; simply confront the alcoholic with the evidence. Inform the executive that it will be handled like any other normal, corporate performance problem and say, "We will have to let you go, unless there is a medical problem associated with your behavior." Then say,

"Of course, the company would prefer to have an evaluation made by its treatment center and an agreement from you to conform with the treatment plan."

Do not let the alcoholic see his own doctor and seek remedy there. Have an established, independent evaluation program arranged by the center or consulting doctor you have selected and insist he submit to this and abide by the treatment recommendations.

Assuming the alcoholic executive submits to the evaluation, and then agrees to the suggested plan of reshaping his life style, you must arrange to have his progress monitored. Be sure the executive realizes that any deviation from the regimen will jeopardize his job.

Initially the alcoholic may not believe that the problem exists, but a good treatment center will usually break down that denial. Normally the job will be more important to the individual than anything else (including the individual's family), and the worthwhile executive will try hard to salvage that career.

Dr. Pace has been treating alcoholism for over 20 years from his office in New York and as medical director for General Motors' New York executive offices.

Criticizing Your Subordinate

By J. Stephen Morris

Criticizing a subordinate can be a real test for even the most seasoned manager. Too often what is supposed to be a constructive session turns into a futile confrontation, with mutual gripes and hard feelings, but no solution of the problem.

Five simple suggestions can help the manager make criticism sessions more productive and problem-solving.

Step 1. Get to the point. Don't evade the issue. Skip the small talk and go straight to the target: "Bob, I want to talk to you about your late reports"; or "Barbara, I called you in to discuss your personality conflict with the director of sales."

This advice appears cold and heartless. You probably feel that a warm and friendly opening, such as, "Bob, how are the kids?" or "Barbara, how's that training for the marathon coming along?" will relax your subordinate and ease the path to solving the problem.

But it rarely works out that way. Stalling and beating around the bush usually only increase the anxieties on both sides.

Step 2. Describe the situation. Use a descriptive opening that is specific, not general. Avoid evaluative openings at all costs.

Evaluative: "Bob, I can no longer deal with your late, sloppy reports." Descriptive: "Bob, you've been late on three reports in the last two weeks. That caused us two shipping delays and cost us $5,000."

Evaluative: "Barbara, you're nasty and abrasive." Descriptive: "Barbara, the sales director has just informed me that you refuse to communicate with him."

Evaluative openings are damaging because they prejudge your subordinate's point of view. This can only pave the way to a confrontation. By being descriptive you set the tone for a factual recounting of the situation *without* prejudging. The subordinate will feel much less threatened, and more willing to cooperate.

Step 3. Use active listening techniques. Encourage the subordinate to tell his side of the story. It will reduce defensiveness, clarify the situation and provide both parties with an opportunity to think the problem through.

It helps to ask open-ended questions that invite discussion, and cannot be answered with a simple "yes" or "no." Begin questions with *what* or *how,* or sometimes *tell me* or *describe.*

Bad: "Do you like our new computer system?" Good: "How do you feel about our new computer system?"

Nodding the head, restating the subordinate's statement in your own words, encouraging more information through silence are other examples of active listening techniques. They invite your subordinate to open up, and reassure him you are interested in and sensitive to his viewpoint.

Step 4. Agree on the source of the problem and its solution. It's essential that the subordinate agree that there is in fact a problem. If he doesn't, there's little likelihood the problem will be solved.

Once you and the subordinate have identified and agreed on the problem, work together to identify the source, and let the subordinate get involved in coming up with a potential solution.

For example, if the problem stems from lack of knowledge, a training program might be the answer. A lack of motivation might be resolved by exploring ways to make the subordinate's job more meaningful or stimulating. If there's a personality conflict between subordinates, you might want to transfer one of them, or get them to work out their difficulties between themselves. You may discover that the subordinate you're criticizing isn't the cause of the problem at all; in that case, you may want to look elsewhere in the chain of command.

No one likes to be ordered around. But by allowing the subordinate to participate in your decisions about resolving a problem, you can be better assured of his active cooperation.

Step 5. Summarize the meeting. Have the subordinate synopsize the discussion and the agreed-upon solution. Both subordinate and manager should leave the session with the same understanding of what was decided. Establish a follow-up date which allows the subordinate reasonable time to correct the situation.

In closing the session, you should reassure the subordinate that you're always available to discuss his progress.

The ultimate measure of your success will be whether the problem that worries you is solved. That's not always possible. But constructive criticism is a skill that can and must be mastered by the manager who is dedicated to improving employee performance, productivity and morale.

Mr. Morris is executive vice president of Drake Beam Morin Inc., an outplacement and human resources management consulting firm.

Criticizing Your Boss

By Hendrie Weisinger and
Norman M. Lobsenz

"Criticize my boss?" "I don't have the right to."
"I'd get fired."
"It's his company, not mine."
Many executives recognize that it's important to encourage criticism from their subordinates. Walking about United Airlines, Ed Carlson solicited criticism, both as a source of information and as a way of conveying respect to middle managers. At ITT, Harold Geneen was well-known for the way he bawled out subordinates, but he also structured the organization to encourage criticism of superiors, including himself. Mr. Geneen felt that criticism of superiors would enable problems to surface more quickly, so they could be nipped in the bud. Konosuke Matsushita built his namesake company with a philosophy stressing criticism as a form of self-discipline necessary to the growth of the individual and the company.

Unfortunately, not everyone has the good fortune to work in such companies. George Steinbrenner, owner of the New York Yankees, is said to have given manager Billy Martin a contract specifically prohibiting him from criticizing his superiors. And the business sections of newspapers and magazines are filled with examples of criticism of top executives with the source consciously being kept anonymous.

If you think things could be improved in your company, but aren't quite sure how your boss will respond to criticism, the following guidelines may be helpful:

1) Make sure it is appropriate to criticize your boss. You must have a direct line of communications to him, and his work must affect your job or the job of your subordinates. It is inappropriate to criticize your superior if his decisions or actions have nothing to do with you.

2) Acknowledge that the boss is the boss, that you are not claiming to be right while he or she is wrong. Any criticism that sets up a power struggle will make your superior more intent on defending his position. Phrase your remarks in a *two-sided solution.* Summarize the situation you believe should be changed; present your criticism as a productive alternative. By offering both sides of the situation you are, in effect, acknowledging your superior's view and defusing his need to defend it. The decision—to make a change or not—is left with the boss.

3) Build the validity of your criticism. By offering it as information you want to share for the common good, you maximize its importance. Cite authoritative sources, submit supporting data from objective and reliable sources. While Mr. Geneen welcomed criticism, he did not suffer fools. He demanded that his people have what he called "unshakable facts." Thus, instead of having to accept or reject a "criticism," your superior is in a position of evaluating material you supplied.

4) Ask for your superior's help in resolving the problem you are calling to his attention. By doing so you will not be "criticizing" your superior, but seeming to criticize yourself by taking responsibility for the "problem." You are making your superior your ally. For example, if your boss is chronically late in providing you with data you need to function effectively, you can say, "I'm having trouble running my department when I don't have the necessary data on time. Can you give me some suggestions for improving this situation?" If your criticism is valid, chances are your superior will "solve the problem"—and resolve the criticism—by meeting his or her deadlines more promptly.

There also may be ways to determine how receptive your superior is to criticism. If he interacts with you outside of structured meetings, and if he is flexible enough to make changes in organizational policy from time to time, he probably tends to see criticism as a source of information rather than as an emotional attack. If your boss keeps to himself and seldom encourages change, criticism will probably not be acceptable, despite its constructive intent, and you will likely be seen as a complainer.

What about those impossible bosses—the ones with short tempers, the ones who "never listen"? Can or should you attempt to offer criticism to them? Only if you can be clever and creative. Gear your strategy to this fundamental question: "How can I communicate this information so that my superior perceives it as being useful?"

Mr. Weisinger, a Santa Monica, Calif., psychologist, and Mr. Lobsenz, a Los Angeles writer, are authors of "Nobody's Perfect: How to Give Criticism and Get Results" (Stratford Press).

Keeping Favoritism and Prejudice Out of Employee Evaluations

By Andrew S. Grove

In my book, "High Output Management," I characterized performance reviews as the single most important form of task-relevant feedback with which we supervisors can provide our employees.

What I said has not been enthusiastically received in all quarters. A teacher friend of mine heatedly insisted that performance reviews—and compensation and promotional practices based on those reviews—would not elicit better work but only favoritism in her school system. Another objection was raised by a lawyer I know who haughtily announced that nobody, simply nobody, could judge the quality of his work. Comments of this type have reached me from other quarters as well.

In spite of the criticisms, I remain steadfast in my conviction that if we want performance in the workplace, somebody has to have the courage and confidence to determine whether we are getting it or not. We must also find ways to enhance what we are getting.

But let's examine these criticisms carefully, taking the lawyer's position first. I am quite sure that in any sizable law firm, an experienced and senior partner can make a meaningful evaluation of my friend's work, no matter how arcane the work might seem. After all, professionals go through intensive series of evaluations during their education. And during their internship, and subsequent professional practice, professionals acquire and share basic facts and values that provide a good basis for meaningful dialogue and mutual evaluation.

This is not to say that when professionals are faced with a complex problem, there is only one way to handle it. Assessing performance is not an *act* but a *process;* even if the opening barrage is off the mark, the resulting exchange is likely to tune and perfect the work performed. In fact, the more obscure and intangible the nature of the work in question, the more such an exchange is likely to contribute to its quality.

For example, some years ago when I was supervising a number of semiconductor engineers, one of them discovered a technique that turned out to be extremely useful in solving an important problem. This solution brought recognition, praise and a lot of satisfaction to my subordinate.

However, as time went on, he fell into the pattern of attempting to solve all problems with this same technique, even though it had no relevance to them. This led to wasted effort and a lot of frustration. When I pointed out this pattern to my subordinate, he got defensive at first. He thought I was trying to minimize the importance of his earlier achievement. As we talked about my observation some more, I eventually succeeded in convincing him that his insistence on using the same technique over and over was counterproductive. Eventually, he managed to break his thinking pattern and address his new problems with a fresh approach each time, thus regaining his earlier effectiveness.

The very idea of non-reviewability of professional work means that only the most monstrous errors get evaluated—after the worst has been perpetrated, and then frequently during the course of malpractice litigation. I think we can reduce the waste and damage caused by this practice in our society by agreeing on a basic principle; namely that *all* work can and must be subjected to review by somebody.

As for the teacher's fear of favoritism, obviously power—

and the right to evaluate *is* power—can corrupt. What we as managers have to do is build enough checks and balances into the system to minimize the influence of personal bias and distortion. At Intel, we use three safeguards.

Once an employee review is written up by a supervisor, the supervisor's boss oversees and approves the written evaluation. This manager is the second most qualified judge of the employee's performance—second, that is, to the employee's immediate supervisor. Being one level removed, he can put the employee's performance in broader perspective; he is in a position to compare it with the work of other people in a larger organization.

Our second check of the evaluation process stipulates that the personnel representative assigned to the employee's department approve the review. Although someone from personnel probably can't judge the quality of highly technical endeavors, he is likely to catch signs of favoritism and prejudice, and call it to the attention of the immediate supervisor's manager. For this to have real effect, we must endow the personnel department with enough status and clout to make its opinions and comments count.

The third check comes from setting up ranking sessions, where the supervisor meets with his peers and, together as a group, they compare and rank all of their subordinates. Of course, no one supervisor can assess the work of all subordinates of his peers. But collectively, enough will be known about each employee to provide additional—and frequently conflicting—points of view to the assessment process, resulting in a fair outcome for everybody.

Do such checks and balances weed out all bad evaluations? They do not. No system is foolproof, especially one that is necessarily laden with human judgment. Furthermore, such an evaluation process takes much more time and effort than simply listing a group of employees by date of hire and letting it go at that (the basis of a seniority approach to evaluating performance). At Intel, we estimate that a supervisor probably spends five to eight hours on each employee's review, about one-quarter to one-third of 1% of the supervisor's work year. If the effort expended contributes to an employee's performance even to a small extent over the course of a year, isn't that a highly worthwhile expenditure of a supervisor's time?

We are paid to manage our organizations. To manage means to elicit better performance from members of our organization. We managers need to stop rationalizing, and to stiffen our resolve and do what we are paid to do.

Mr. Grove is president of Intel Corp. in Santa Clara, Calif., and is the author of "High Output Management" (Random House, 1983).

How to Live With Those Mercurial Mavericks

By James E. Seitz

The toughest challenge for leaders of professional service organizations is managing creative thinkers who don't always abide by the rules. Professionals on the leading edge of their specialties tend to be mavericks who don't succumb easily to standard management approaches.

The term maverick comes from the legendary Texan nonconformist, Samuel Maverick, who broke the established code of the West by refusing to brand his calves. It's an apt description for many of the professionals who make unique and vital contributions to service firms—the advertising copywriter who composes unorthodox but memorable commercials, the attorney whose knowledge of law and human nature is extremely valuable for corporate acquisitions; or the tax accountant who consistently develops profitable and previously unrecognized tax strategies for corporations.

Such people often believe that it is unnecessary to follow the rules as long as they produce results. They have high standards for their own work, and they can be extraordinarily industrious. But at times they usurp authority and even ignore, finesse or sabotage conventional management systems. They also can be abrupt and impatient with those who don't see the world as they do. They feel the organization is there to serve them.

Professional mavericks want to be free enough to put

their high energy to good use. Management should want the same result. But in an organization, even those mavericks who do superior work have to be managed. The task requires a unique combination of support and control.

Support can mean help on administrative details such as time-and-expense reports, research assistance, paperwork and follow-up. Even mavericks must see to it that reports are prepared and records kept, but good staff help can free them from workloads that clutter the job.

Emotional and financial support are paramount as well. Mavericks can get discouraged easily, and often support means giving ground to compensate for their emotional highs and lows. Creative thinkers are natural risk-takers and, unfortunately, this produces failure as well as success. Here, positive reinforcement is vital.

I have found that taking the time to sit down and talk, usually initiating the conversations—rarely scheduling them—demonstrates the real personal interest of management. With management support, a true maverick will bounce back after failure and chase after the next goal with renewed innovation and daring. Giving your good people the assurance needed when tackling a bold project and endorsing the commitment with budget dollars for a future payoff are crucial.

Controls should center on those areas where the maverick might overdo it—especially overemphasis on a pet research area or activity that isn't feasible for the company. It's difficult but necessary to "reason together" in these situations, listening, explaining your thought process so that you can conclude on a positive note even when you don't agree.

Self-starters, high achievers and innovators don't need to be subjected to work measurement or time utility systems. But they usually do need control over expenses, since they tend to be extravagant or, at best, untidy.

Yet controls shouldn't undercut the mavericks' motivation. In professional service organizations, where innovation can make the difference between success and failure, it's important to remember that motivation produces productivity and control simply measures it.

I make two pacts with mavericks. The first is that I'll support their frontier efforts if they keep me informed. Surprises, of course, cannot be managed after the fact. Too many surprises can cause the course of an organization to alter. The second is that I'll let them deviate from the strict letter of the administrative manual if, in the process, they don't abuse other members of the organization.

Mavericks can be hard to live with. Those who don't fit the maverick mold, who do a job well without needing or demanding a rule-breaking license, must be assuaged and properly rewarded. They must be aware of the unique contribution of the stars. But just as Reggie Jackson isn't going to get very far without the sustained support of good fielders, fine pitching and effective management, the overall company effort must function as a cohesive unit. One star may get more headlines and money but a good manager knows the value and contribution of each player.

As a manager of professional mavericks, I don't always get to my "to do" list. This is because the watches of mavericks don't tick at a steady rate. They aren't time wasters, they just use time differently. Deadlines are important but each minute doesn't have the same value. Mavericks place a great deal of value on conversation where they either dispense insight or at times gain insight.

It doesn't take long to learn that professional mavericks are an interesting breed. We talk about new ideas, new concepts and the attendant investment risks associated with the yet undone. Like the cartoon character Available Jones in "L'il Abner," I answer yes when mavericks ask, "Are you available, Available?" Managing them, working with them, is fun.

Mr. Seitz is partner-in-charge of the New York office of Touche Ross & Co. and is a director of Touche Ross and Touche Ross International.

Never Coddle a Malcontent

By Peter Baida

Managers learn from many unlikely sources, but few sources would seem less likely than the fiction of an author whom we associate with monomaniacal sea captains and voyages to metaphysical seas.

Amazingly, Herman Melville left us not only the finest novel ever written about a whaling voyage but also the finest story ever written about a business office. The story is called "Bartleby the Scrivener: A Story of Wall Street," and its subject is employee relations—specifically, the relationship between a baffled manager and a staggeringly rebellious subordinate.

"Bartleby" was published in 1853 in Putnam's Monthly Magazine and reprinted three years later in Melville's only volume of short fiction, "The Piazza Tales." Already famous as "the man who lived among the cannibals," the 34-year-old author took his readers on a journey to a world as exotic as the South Sea islands he had celebrated in "Typee" and "Omoo"—the world of a law firm in lower Manhattan.

The story made no great impression upon Melville's contemporaries: To judge from their memoirs, businessmen of the 19th century read little except the Bible and "The Autobiography of Benjamin Franklin." In the 20th century, the literary critics and scholars who rescued Melville from oblivion have tended to emphasize meanings that lie below the surface in "Bartleby," but they have missed the surface itself. They have missed the point that "Bartleby" is, above all, a story about business.

The narrator introduces himself as "one of those unambitious lawyers who never address a jury, or in any way draw down public applause; but, in the cool tranquility of a snug retreat, do a snug business among rich men's bonds, and mortgages, and title-deeds"—in short, a man who has based his life upon "a profound conviction that the easiest way of life is the best."

This placid gentleman manages a staff of three in an office "not . . . very arduous, but very pleasantly remunerative." His troubles begin when business takes so sharp a turn for the better that he finds it necessary to enlarge his staff.

Enter Bartleby—"a motionless young man . . . . pallidly neat, pitiably respectable, incurably forlorn"—exactly the job applicant who will command the interest of a manager whose deepest motive and desire, no matter what else he might say, is to find a candidate who will not make trouble.

Bartleby begins as an exemplary employee: "As if long famishing for something to copy, he seemed to gorge himself on my documents." What more could a manager want, especially when the new employee combines such commendable productivity with a character "so singularly sedate"?

A manager may expect the rebellion of a disgruntled, immature or hot-headed employee, but few managers ever expect the rebellion of a reliable employee. In Bartleby's case, the rebellion comes without warning, and it announces itself "in a singularly mild, firm voice, . . . [without] the least uneasiness, anger, impatience, or impertinence." There is no provocation. On a day like any other day, the attorney gives an order like any other order and receives in return the astounding reply, "I would prefer not to."

Unlike a modern manager, the manager in "Bartleby" cannot consult any of 10,000 guides on "How to Handle the Problem Employee." He must rely upon his own instincts and experience, but nothing in his experience has prepared him for a gentle rebel. "I was turned into a pillar of salt, standing at the head of my seated column of clerks."

Even in circumstances that he regards as "unprecedented and violently unreasonable," a good manager will not rush to judgment. The "wonderful mildness" of Bartleby, the utter absence of anything that resembles insolence or hostility, causes his employer to tolerate behavior that he would not accept of a subordinate who displayed the least hint of animosity.

Any manager who has wavered over the fate of a marginal employee will sympathize with Melville's narrator as he flounders in an agony of indecision and rationalization. Irritation at the challenge to his authority is softened by pity and an appreciation of Bartleby's value to the business: "Poor fellow! thought I, he means no mischief;... He is useful to me. I can get along with him."

But the list of tasks that Bartleby prefers not to undertake grows steadily longer, and the manager finds himself scheming to provoke the outright defiance that would justify outright dismissal. A trivial order is given, the clerk prefers not to comply and the manager imagines that the moment of truth has arrived:

"You *will* not?"

"I *prefer* not."

And so it goes. Bartleby never refuses, but he prefers not to proofread his copy, prefers not to run errands, prefers not to say anything that might clarify or justify his rebellion. Asked to be "a little reasonable," he answers honestly that "[a]t present I would prefer not to be a little reasonable." At last he announces that he prefers to do no more copying—prefers to do no work at all.

The bafflement of the manager in this encounter is the bafflement of a business mind brought into contact with a mind that declines to attend to business. But it is more. It is the bafflement of a good man—a reasonable, civilized and charitable man—brought into contact with a spirit of suicidal negation. The comedy moves inexorably to a tragic conclusion.

In the end, reasoning that "[s]ince he will not quit me, I

must quit him," the attorney moves his office to another location. Evicted by the new landlord, Bartleby "persists in haunting the building generally," until at last he is imprisoned as a vagrant. In jail, predictably, he prefers not to eat, though the attorney bribes a jailer to bring him food. As others might succumb to age or disease, Bartleby succumbs to his preferences.

Bartleby is a pure type—the perfect embodiment of what the 20th century has come to call "a negative attitude." No guidance or counseling could save him; no modern principles of enlightened personnel management could make any difference for him. In the end, his employer can only sigh, "Ah, Bartleby! Ah, humanity!" It is a sad story with a wealth of meaning, but for managers the lesson is clear. Never coddle a malcontent.

Mr. Baida is deputy director of development at Memorial Sloan-Kettering Cancer Center.

The Younger Boss: Green Over Gray Needn't Lead to a Clash

By Marilyn Machlowitz

Authority has long been associated with age. So executives and professionals who supervise people older than themselves face a special kind of management challenge.

A youthful college president attended his first meeting of a prestigious educational association. His counterparts mistook him for a waiter.

An international lawyer looked so young that opposing counsel assumed she was a secretary. They handed her some critical documents to photocopy.

It's usually best for the young executive not to make much of a fuss about such embarrassing incidents. Sometimes it is even possible to turn them to one's advantage: The lawyer wished she had been given more sensitive documents to copy.

But aside from being mistaken for a "gofer," the young manager must learn how to assert his authority when he doesn't fully look the part. Since authority has also been associated with sex, young woman bosses operate against a double whammy. Such expressions as "fair-haired boy" have few feminine equivalents.

Some young bosses try to appear older. Clothes do the trick for some, while the "boy wonder" beard works for others. These can be a disservice, however, if they only emphasize the person's youth because of the contrast to his countenance.

Others flaunt their youth, mentioning it before anyone else can as a sort of preemptive strike. Youth offers some protection in that even ordinary performance may be judged extraordinary for someone who is a mere 22. But this defense calls into question one's legitimacy as a decision maker and supervisor.

Perhaps the greatest danger is an inconsistency that confuses subordinates. As the young person inexperienced at exercising authority experiments, he may overdo it on occasion and then back off to compensate. Unsure of how to behave, he may unwittingly reduce his legitimate authority by trying to be overly chummy or by retreating to the role of a precocious child.

A second problem for young bosses is finding peers. Contemporaries may be several levels lower and counterparts may be 20 years older. Peer support is helpful both personally and professionally, and the young high achiever makes a mistake if he places a high value on seeming self-sufficient and has trouble seeking assistance. At the same time, some senior people may feel threatened by the younger person's rate of progress and be reluctant to assist anyone who seems to be advancing very well as it is.

In such circumstances, it often helps to seek superiors, sponsors or friends who have enjoyed similar fast starts. Such people probably won't feel any need to show you a thing or two to put you in your place, and may extend themselves. Alair Townsend held responsible positions while still in her 20s. Now older and budget director for New York City, she is said to have organized lunch-time seminars for bright young people on her staff to keep them involved, interested and informed.

The mere presence of a young new boss creates ripples throughout a department. These seem to occur in the following sequence. The first is psychological: Your older subordinates' pride is hurt. The second is political: They feel you may be blocking their paths. The third is practical: They worry that your knowledge and values may be a generation apart from theirs.

These reactions are understandable, and there may not be much you can do about them initially. It's important to recognize, however, that any animosity isn't directed at you personally. So don't be defensive.

At the same time, don't come on like Gangbusters. Don't hide your expertise, but don't boast about it either or others will try to knock you off the pedestal. When Michael Weisman became an associate producer at NBC Sports at 24, he says, he made a point not to "come in and start pushing people around. I came in very humble and was very appreciative of whatever they could add."

Don't behave as though you're just passing through. It can rile your staff to think that the position that might be the capstone of their careers is just a stepping stone for you.

Extend yourself to others, especially if you come in from outside. When Donna Shalala became president of Hunter College in her 30s, she reportedly went to meet faculty members in their own offices, instead of asking them to come to hers. Be tactful. Don't refer to those who've labored long and hard for your company by such derogatory terms as "lifers" or "old-timers."

Don't assume that problems have to develop. Such situations may be hard, but they need not be horrid. T. George Harris, editor-in-chief of American Health magazine, is 26 years older than his publisher and boss, Owen Lipstein. Mr. Harris explains: "Time and time again, there are things I want to try out that most publishers would say 'No' to, but we work them out." His conclusion? "Owen is the best publisher I've ever worked with."

Ms. Machlowitz, a New York personnel consultant, is author of "Workaholics" and the forthcoming "Whiz Kids: Success at an Early Age." Arbor House, 1985.

The Proper Distance Between Boss and Secretary

By Mortimer R. Feinberg and
Aaron Levenstein

Most executives depend on their secretaries in two crucial ways. A good secretary makes sure her boss functions efficiently. (Despite the return of the male secretary, the present ratio of the sexes justifies use of the female personal pronoun.) She keeps his desk organized, plans his time, shields him from debilitating interruptions, makes sure nothing goes out over his signature that will embarrass him and keeps him apprised of scuttlebutt picked up in the ladies' room.

More significant may be the emotional support she gives him in times of crisis. This may prove even more helpful than the traditional secretarial duties, especially in the event of corporate infighting or economic setbacks for the company. Nevertheless, it is important for both executive and secretary that some distance be kept between them. The secretary owes her primary loyalty to the company that pays her—not to the individual. She should not be involved in discussions with an outside headhunter or otherwise put in a compromising position where her loyalty to company and boss will conflict. As the chief executive officer of a large conglomerate put it:

"The personal tie may make her vulnerable in the event that you retire or leave for another job. Never force her to choose between her commitment to you and her duty to the company. You have no right to expect her to throw herself on the funeral pyre like a Hindu widow committing *suttee.*"

One of the purposes of a secretary is to relieve the executive of personal burdens and thus reduce pressure on his work. Contrary to feminist ideology, it is not demeaning for a secretary to prepare coffee, order sandwiches, etc. if she has been given to understand in the hiring interview that such personal services are part of her job. The executive can demonstrate that, in his view, the chore is not demeaning by doing the pouring himself from time to time.

But it is still important for the executive to draw a clear line between private and corporate functions. Your secretary shouldn't be required to handle personal checks, bank accounts, tax deductions, intimate personal correspondence and so on, except possibly in rare emergencies, such as illness in the family. The relationship will be contaminated if limits are left undefined.

When the executive wants a secretary who can listen to his woes and who will allow him to unload on her the pressures of the moment, the selection procedure is of the utmost importance. Interviewing, testing and checking of experience must be addressed to finding a mature person who can cope with stress. This type of secretary is likely to be qualified to serve as a chief of staff. In that case, she must be given appropriate assistance so that she is not overwhelmed by the daily chores of correspondence and telephone calls. She might even be given stock options and other management perks.

Even though you consider your secretary a confidante, she should not be involved in the factional conflicts of the organization. Don't make her listen to your invidious comments about your peers, superiors or subordinates. As one executive told us: "I have to exercise restraint to avoid burdening my secretary with uncomplimentary characterizations of associates. That is unprofessional: She may overhear arguments or abusive exchanges, and she knows where I stand, but I don't make her a captive audience for my hostilities."

Keep in mind that you are a role model to your subordinates, including your secretary. Be scrupulous in your behavior. Don't ask her to be a party to an abuse of the expense account. The executive who tells his secretary to put in a voucher for a nonbusiness lunch with friends right after using a fine-toothed comb on the vouchers of his subordinates generates cynicism and disrespect.

Many jokes in bad taste purport to describe the hostility of executives' wives and secretaries. The most famous example of such tension is the case of Mrs. Roosevelt and FDR's secretary, Missy LeHand. Joseph P. Lash, in his biography "Eleanor and Franklin," cites a journalist's description of "how Missy presided over the White House tea table when Mrs. Roosevelt was not there, how she wrote all of the president's private letters, did the accounts, paid the bills, balanced his checkbooks, saw that the children got their personal allowances, kept track of his stamp, marine-print, and rare-book collections, and ran the Little White House at Warm Springs 'when Mrs. Roosevelt can't be there.'"

These services, says Mr. Lash, were "beyond price" and helped the president immensely. But that his family paid a price is evidenced by the resentful statements of his children years later, though Mrs. Roosevelt herself suffered the displacement in silence. The executive who seeks to maintain a wholesome marriage should not permit his secretary to invade the prerogatives and functions of his spouse.

The extension of anti-discrimination laws to cover "sexual harassment" now adds a legal as well as moral deterrent to taking advantage of one's position as employer. Such misconduct is defined by the Equal Employment Opportunity Commission to "include unwelcome sexual advances, requests for sexual favors and other verbal or physical conduct of a sexual nature."

The term "verbal conduct" covers unwelcome off-color or suggestive remarks. A fairly typical policy statement by a Midwestern manufacturing company warns that management will not tolerate "solicitation, insults, comments, jokes, verbal or physical advances or other sexually based activities." Aware that such prohibitions exist, the executive must be sure to draw a line between coarseness and humor. When in doubt, self-censorship is the best policy. A respectful informality is a sound basis for a dignified and yet relaxed relationship. The individual who is all work and no play rarely pauses to notice his secretary's attractive new hairdo or to make comments like, "Where did you get that dress—from the Salvation Army?" A continuing relationship requires some element of lightness from time to time.

The executive must remember that every human relationship—even with one's spouse and children at home, but certainly with one's subordinates on the job—should not be all-consuming. The warmest of relationships will ultimately chill unless a certain area of individual privacy is reserved.

Finally, it should be noted that the executive has no claim to total and absolute commitment in what is, after all, an economic relationship. He must avoid fantasizing that he is emotionally indispensable to his secretary, and that she will dedicate herself single-mindedly to his needs.

Mr. Feinberg is chairman of BFS Psychological Associates, a New York consulting firm. Mr. Levenstein is professor emeritus of management at Baruch College.

Meeting With Success

By Jack Falvey

"Is this meeting necessary?" is a question that should be asked far more frequently in organizations. Few managers understand the dynamics of meetings. Meetings are best used to ratify and build on decisions already made, not to hammer out policies in a group grope environment. Surprises are best left to birthday parties. Effective meetings require that all participants have detailed advance information on what their roles involve and what is to be accomplished overall.

If your last stop before going into a meeting is at the photocopier to run off your agenda, stop right there and either cancel or reschedule the gathering. What rational manager would undertake a business trip on the spur of the moment without an itinerary or pre-arranged appointments and a set of desired results? Accepting minimal results from uninformed or hastily informed meeting participants is a gross waste of management time.

The only reason to ask people to attend a meeting is so that they can personally contribute. If they will not be asked to contribute, don't ask them to come. Send them the results after the meeting and a great deal of time and expense will be saved.

NCR's John Patterson, the father of the modern sales

meeting, brought his sales force together so the juniors could meet and see what made his top producers successful. The stars came to share techniques, and everyone else—including top management—came to learn. Which leads us to perhaps the most important feature of any sales meeting: to provide recognition for top performance. This should be done two ways. First, make sure that your stars have substantive, well-produced contributions to make to the program. Second, make sure that your formal recognition ceremonies take place at the beginning, not the end, of your meeting. Let the light shine as long as possible on those who deserve it, and give everyone else a chance for maximum adoration, questions and envy.

Be sure your awards are high in recognition value. Joke gifts of any kind are inappropriate. But investments in symbolic hardware pay dividends all out of proportion to cost. The master's green jacket or the championship ring are examples of this concept.

Frances Rubacha, director of sales for Radio City Music Hall Productions, gets involved in putting on major meetings for her clients both in New York and in the field. She says managers must realize when dealing with groups that all the rules of theater arts apply. To disregard them will result in less than optimum effects. A few examples:

• Putting people in a darkened room and running 20 slide projectors at once may create a certain spectacle, but the sales people who build the top line on the income statement each month deserve much more.

• Puppet, football and mountain-climbing films have been overdone. Few sales organizations are asked to climb mountains or win football games.

• The eight-hour day may be fine for your factory, but audience-oriented activities don't work well in excess of two or three hours. Less is actually better. Well-produced, fast-moving, brief general sessions are the rule to work toward.

• Running passive, one-way sessions for more than 30 minutes just about guarantees poor results. Everyone must be involved constantly.

• Little exercises or breakout sessions are superficial at

best. They are no substitute for well-planned activities that all participants can prepare for well in advance of the meeting itself.

Ms. Rubacha suggests that each meeting segment be taken as a half-day selling segment that must answer the attendees' constant questions of: Why should I listen to this? What's in it for me if I do? And, what should I do as a result of all this?

Taking your sales team to a resort location for three days and allowing half a day for recreation is not the best strategy. (It usually rains on the day off anyway.) By running half-day or midday general sessions and promoting informal gatherings during extended use of the resort facilities, you will obtain far better returns than from the traditional 8 a.m. to 8 p.m. marathon meetings.

People must know what is expected of them in advance and in detail. Each attendee at a meeting should have a set of written objectives approved by his or her line manager before leaving for a meeting.

If the president or chairman of the board attends your meeting, be sure to give him or her a set of objectives as well. Don't let the chief executive officer fly in on the corporate jet, deliver a one-hour speech, and then fly away again. Insist that top management attend the full program. If the top executives must come by corporate jet, have them fly around and pick up your top sales producers on the way. If they want to give a big speech, have it printed up in advance and send copies out to everyone. See if you can use a news conference type of format, with both pre-submitted anonymous questions raised by the speech's content and a chance for audience participation. What better investment of top management's time than formal and extended informal meetings with field personnel?

When an acquaintance was president of his own medical equipment company in Wilmington, Mass., he used to prepare his remarks on flip charts weeks in advance of his national sales meeting. Anyone who walked by his office was asked to come in and look over the charts and hear the details of his message.

He went over his presentation literally hundreds of times before he took it on stage. The results showed. He made dynamic, flawless presentations that carried each and every point beautifully.

One last word on formal program length. Never forget that the Gettysburg Address was in fact delivered by Edward Everett, who spoke for one hour on the significance of the event of the day. Lincoln was merely asked to say a few words to close the program.

Mr. Falvey is a management consultant in Londonderry, N.H., who speaks (briefly) at sales meetings. He wrote and produced the film "Session One."

The Transforming Leader

By Mortimer R. Feinberg and
Aaron Levenstein

"You deliver for me, and I'll deliver for you." That's one type of leadership. Historian and political analyst James Mac-Gregor Burns defines such leadership as "transactional." In his book "Leadership," Mr. Burns devotes several hundred pages to the differences between a run-of-the-mill "transactional" leader and what he calls an exceptional, charismatic, "transforming" leader.

In the transactional relationship, the end result is a "payoff." In the transforming relationship, the end result is a substantial change in the subordinate: personal growth. The former provides only material reward; the latter provides psychic income.

Gen. George C. Marshall advised his colleagues to develop people toward self-reliance. "If you want a man to be for you," he said, "never let him feel he is dependent on you. Make him feel you are in some way dependent on him." And the best way to do that is to teach him to stand on his own feet.

The would-be transforming leader does not always succeed. Some people are unalterably dependent and incapable of growth. As one cynic puts it, "You can't grow grass on concrete." We talked with executives who saw themselves as the beneficiaries of such leadership. They describe their

experiences in terms that lend themselves to six impera-
tives:

1) *Show a personal interest in individual progress.* The
transforming leader studies and understands his people,
knowing not only their current abilities but their potential.
Lyman Wood, president of Brennan College Services Inc.,
says the transforming leader pushes people beyond the
threshold of their self-imposed limits toward their own un-
realized potential.

Unquestionably the transforming leader must begin with
a sound knowledge of the employee's character and potential. Elwood L. LaForge Jr., corporate group vice president
of Lenox Inc., recalls an executive who helped shape his
career: "He always gave me enough rope to show what I
had, but never enough to hang myself. And he was always
there with the lifeline when I needed it."

2) *Build charismatic relationships.* The term charisma
derives from a Greek word representing a divine element
and therefore is beyond definition. But the behavior of the
charismatic leader can be described: He creates confidence
in his judgment, competence and good will. Followers identify with him. They feel they can be sure of his availability
when they need him. He makes tasks interesting, exudes
purposefulness, generates a feeling of venturesomeness and
stirs excitement.

He is not necessarily humorous or intellectual, but he is
personable. People like to be with him because he respects
their individuality. But most important, he sets an example
that others want to emulate.

3) *Encourage other people to shine.* The transforming
leader keeps them on a loose rein, even though he expects
them to commit some errors as part of the growth process.

The effective leader looks for opportunities to express sin-
cere appreciation. One executive recalls the thrill he experienced when his superior congratulated him on his skill in
selecting subordinates: "Where did you get Stevens? He's a
real find!"

E. Garrett Bewkes Jr., chairman of American Bakeries
Co., warns against what he terms "the counterfeit trans-

forming leader." In one way or another, "he makes you want to break your back on his behalf, but after you've been with him a month you find it's all facade and he doesn't really sustain the role."

4) *Provide psychological support.* To turn the transactional relationship into a transforming experience, the leader must make a conscious effort to elevate the subordinate. The objective is to raise the individual's level of aspirations and strengthen self-confidence.

Robert A. M. Coppenrath, president of Agfa-Gevaert Inc., puts it this way: "The transforming leader, as you call him, removes fear. It's like a frog in the pond; the leader gets the frog to make the jump."

But the effect may well be to spread illusions if all the leader does is to raise sights and inflate confidence. He must also raise the individual's ability to perform. That is why an additional step must be taken: The leader must instruct, provide training and facilities, and improve the conditions in which the tasks are to be performed.

5) *Ask questions—but in a special way.* The purpose is to draw out more of what the individual has in him. Walter Liss, president of the Broadcast division of Cox Communications Inc., recalling what his mentor did for him, emphasizes the distinction:

"The questions are not designed just to find out what you know, but to stimulate you to explore new options. The questions that made a difference to me were like the work of a cubist painter who forces you simultaneously to look at every side of the object. The questions must be such that they don't allow you to settle for the obvious."

6) *Keep people informed.* The purpose is not just to load them with more facts, relevant and irrelevant, but to enlarge their perception and get them to explore further.

Thus, the transforming leader gets his followers to look at problems from a fresh angle and with new purposes. This requires that he keep his people informed about his own values and priorities.

In the real world, however, no leader can afford to be Johnny-One-Note. There are times when he must be transactional: People do have a right to expect material rewards for services rendered. Moreover, issues of status may make a difference. The pressures of daily life may permit the executive to be transforming with his immediate staff and compel him to be more transactional with people down the line or out in the field. But the awareness of what style he is practicing, and under what circumstances, will enhance his leadership skills.

The rewards of transforming leadership are many. President Truman, who acknowledged such leadership in his general, George Marshall, said of him: "I sincerely hope that when it comes my time to cross the great river, Marshall will place me on his staff, so that I may try to do for him what he did for me."

Mr. Feinberg is chairman of BFS Psychological Associates, a New York consulting firm. Mr. Levenstein is professor emeritus of management at Baruch College.

4

Strategy

The Risks and Advantages of Cooperative Ventures

By Robert J. Conrads
and Amir Mahini

As the GM-Toyota plan to produce automobiles jointly in California gets under way, it may be a good time to ask how important these joint ventures are and whether we will see even more of them. Was our director in Tokyo, Ken Ohmae, right when he observed recently in The Asian Wall Street Journal that "reality is taking the form of joint collaboration, not antagonistic confrontation"? Will the metaphors of war that characterize our business jargon give way to a new language of cooperation?

Today, it's not unusual to see a company such as Burroughs using various partnerships to access Hitachi's technology, package Fujitsu's high-speed facsimile machines and manufacture Nippon Electric's optical readers. Full-page ads have announced that "AT&T and Phillips are venturing forth together." IBM shared a booth with Rolm at an important industry trade show in Geneva to dramatize their linkup. Companies in steel, autos, electronics, chemicals, even biotechnology find themselves involved in spiderwebs of consortia.

Nevertheless, it is not an easy decision to team up. In the aerospace industry, for example, one of the most attractive markets is Japan, but cracking that market may require teaming up with a Japanese company. If patterns hold,

131

the Japanese company may acquire technology from its partner and also become a world-wide competitor, further crowding the market. Is it better to pursue a relationship with a future competitor or wait for a consortium to attack you while you play singly in a doubles match?

Many matchings have failed. For the last several years low-cost parts and labor have led to joint U.S.-Japan partnerings. In several cases the Japanese companies have acquired U.S. technology and knowledge of the American market and then ended the relationship. Such was the case with Ricoh-Savin. So, too, with Pentax and Honeywell, Canon and Bell & Howell.

A bigger problem for American and European firms is that they have tended to sell marketing and distribution cheaply, especially in segments where the technology and components their partners offered have become less important relative to service and dependability. There have been some cases where a company with good marketing sought a partner with state-of-the-art products but examined only its current lineup of hardware, looking for a quick fix to a product line problem. It's the engineering and development talent, of course, that will produce the next two or three generations of products, and this may be the real value to search for in a relationship. Once you find it, however, making the partnership work in the face of engineering's natural "not-invented-here" attitude and day-to-day operating demands isn't easy.

Despite the risks, arguments for cooperation are still strong. Companies are teaming up on product development because costs have become enormous—over half a billion dollars for a central-office switch and investments in large computers. Or they are turning to marketing arrangements to ensure sufficient sales world-wide to justify these investments. More recently they have been teaming up in production to gain scale advantages. In part that's why Alfa-Romeo and Nissan are jointly producing car engines in southern Italy.

Other factors appear to be at work, as well. As technology merges products and markets in some segments of electronics, customers have stopped buying stand-alone products in favor of systems of hardware and software. Companies have to provide everything—hardware, software, sales, service and technology—to compete. As a result, those with superior technology are cooperating with companies that excel in marketing and sales experience.

Organizational as well as strategic issues sometimes argue for partnerships. Our partner, Bob Waterman, in his book "In Search of Excellence" noted that some of America's most successful companies keep things small by limiting the size of their divisions, research departments and plants. Scale advantages cannot, however, be ignored. By being imaginative in pursuing scale outside the company through partner arrangements, management may be able to keep things small and specialized within. Farming out those elements of production that are susceptible to scale advantage, they can stay focused on those factors that differentiate their products and lead to wider margins.

The question sometimes isn't whether to form a partnership, but how long to engage in it. There are good reasons to stay flexible, even when a partnership is working well. New products, technologies and channels may make a partner less valuable. The classic example is the rise of large department and discount store chains in the U.S. that helped Japanese TV set makers go direct rather than supply U.S. original equipment manufacturers.

Not all partnerships need to be short-term, but the secret to long-term success seems to be that each partner invest in key functions and not depend totally on the other. Kawasaki, initially weak in the technology of automation equipment, has invested to catch up with its partner, Unimation, and now exports world-wide through Unimation's network.

Because a partner may some day be a competitor, he must be watched. Investments in R&D and capacity may tip off his intentions and options. Upstream partners can be stalled from selling directly by building in incentives to insure customer loyalty and being smart about the family of products offered.

It's important to be more than fairly represented on the

management team of the joint enterprise, control market planning, have access to sales information and work out the details of how technology will be shared. Montedison and Hercules had announced that they are teaming up in a joint venture involving plastics and pharmaceutical production. The plastics operation will use high-yield technology jointly developed by Montedison and a Japanese competitor. Friend today, foe tomorrow.

Mr. Conrads is a principal in McKinsey & Co.'s Los Angeles office and heads the firm's electronics practice. Mr. Mahini is a senior research consultant in McKinsey's international strategy group.

Test Marketing: Your Product May Do Better Without It

By Solomon Dutka
and Richard L. Lysaker

The mortality rate of new products is high. Existing products face a constant threat of losing momentum and market share. To address both of these problems, companies invest many millions of dollars each year in test marketing.

For both new and established products, test marketing in a limited geographical area, before "going national," is an effective way to examine the performance of marketing variables. It is useful in determining the best advertising theme, spending level, media mix and pricing strategy. Results can show whether advertising goals are being met, a couponing program is effective, in-store displays are being utilized and to what extent a new product will bring additional sales vs. "cannibalizing" sales of the company's existing products. Market tests also enable a company to anticipate competitive response and get a head start on formulating post-introductory strategy.

Test marketing is not just a matter of finding out whether consumers will repurchase a product once they have tried it. It also concerns why they will do so, and how the product should be positioned to achieve maximum sales. Does it have the right name, packaging and price? Is it aimed at the right market segment? What is the best distribution strategy? Knowing the answers to these and other questions can enable adjustments that spell the difference between success and failure.

Yet there are times when test marketing is unwarranted, just as there are circumstances when it would be hazardous to proceed without it. Knowing the difference is important because the wrong decision can prove costly in money or time—and usually both.

The bulk of new-product test marketing is conducted on additions or adjustments to current lines, because this is where competition is most intense, product introductions are most numerous, and market fragmentation is most severe. In some cases, however, it is overdone because managers who are reluctant to make decisions have gotten into the habit of using test marketing as "extra insurance" when it is not really necessary.

A revolutionary new product that offers obvious advantages is apt not to require a market test. Testing also is not practical for products with high capital costs and long lead times in development, such as automobiles and refrigerators, or for those sensitive to time factors and advancing technology, such as fashions and home computers.

Test marketing is not an exercise to be carried out routinely or as a matter of custom. It is generally inadvisable or unwarranted when:

• The product has a short or seasonal selling period or limited life span.

• Disclosure of the product in a test market would deprive the company of an important competitive edge because the product can be quickly duplicated.

• The expense of conducting a test outweighs the risk of going into broad distribution.

• The product is considered a necessary response to a move by competitors.

• Market conditions are changing so fast that results of a market test could prove to be invalid.

In practice, testing is inversely related to the price of a product, but positively related to the frequency of purchase. More can be learned about high-volume, low-cost products than in those cases where purchase cycles are long. Test marketing for these latter cases becomes either impractical or very costly, sometimes prohibitively so. This is because data on repurchase rates are critical in measuring future sales potential.

Testing a product in a limited market is often expensive, involving significant marketing costs, store auditing and consumer research as well. Some companies with a regular flow of new products attempt to reduce these costs through controlled store testing, which limits the need for a full test market and diversion of the regular sales force. This approach concentrates on a limited number of stores for in-depth measurement of the impact of a number of marketing and product variables, such as pricing, couponing and displays. This type of test can be carried out by a research organization that takes total responsibility for obtaining distribution of the test product, restocking store shelves, measuring sales and even providing warehousing and billing procedures.

Of course, there is no way to predetermine perfectly that a new product or marketing program will be a success, no matter how much research is done. The question is how much information or evidence management needs for decision making. While test marketing is crucial in many cases, it could prove wasteful and even counterproductive in others.

Mr. Dutka is chief executive officer and Mr. Lysaker is president of Audits & Surveys Inc., a major marketing research firm based in New York.

Corporate Planning Needn't Be a Straitjacket

By John M. Stengrevics

Corporate planning is getting a bad name these days. Many companies with sophisticated planning systems have been caught off guard by unforeseen events, such as political upheavals or changes in oil prices or moves by their competitors. But formal planning does have its place in today's business environment—so long as one doesn't expect too much of it. Furthermore, the best planning usually takes place outside of a formal planning structure.

There are three major criticisms of formal planning as practiced. First, a formal plan put together once a year quickly can be overtaken by events. Assumptions that once seemed reasonable turn out, in retrospect, to be ludicrous. Any company in the last few years that based its plan on a continuing shortage of oil appreciates this. However, it isn't always fair to blame corporate planners for misjudging the future. The Central Intelligence Agency didn't accurately foresee the Iranian revolution. Could Bechtel or other companies doing business in Iran forecast what the CIA could not?

The second criticism of formal planning is not often talked about openly. Plans that specify changes in the allocation of capital resources among businesses (among "cash cows," "stars," and "dogs" in planning parlance) also signal the rise and fall of the managers in charge of those businesses. From a political point of view, it just isn't feasible to put the "real" plan on paper and casually circulate it through the distribution list. At least not without taking steps to lessen the unwanted effects on status and careers.

Finally, there is the gulf between the designers of the planning system (staff) and the line managers who have to make it happen. Planning staffers often are relatively young MBAs who, although intelligent and well-educated, lack experience. They also have their own objectives, for which they can't be blamed, but which do differ from those of the line managers their planning systems are supposed to serve.

These are valid criticisms. However, they must be weighed against the potential benefits of strategic planning. In a work environment, where day-to-day pressures are extremely demanding, formal planning systems *require* managers to devote time to thinking about the future of their businesses. As a supplement to "gut feel," formal systems constitute an analytical, rigorous and methodical approach to organization.

Of course, the best planning often isn't formal at all, but it does involve strategic thinking. Alfred P. Sloan Jr., General Motors' chief executive from 1923 to 1946, has been given much of the credit for developing a strategy that carried GM to pre-eminence in the automobile industry. The strategy consisted of making available different models priced to appeal to different consumer segments. They were positioned to overlap so that practically all of the buying public—from the most price conscious to the most affluent—was covered. The plan encompassed integrated production and assembly lines, but with a greater degree of flexibility than that which was practiced at archrival Ford. Interestingly enough, Mr. Sloan devised this powerful strategy without the benefit of a formal planning system.

Many managers I have talked with agree that, like Mr. Sloan's, many of their best strategies are carried around with them in their heads. For example, having presided over the development of a process that produced extremely fine metal fibers, one manager was assigned the task of establishing a business unit that was to supply manufacturers of filtration equipment. Some time later, noting that demand was considerably short of what the corporation had come to expect, he changed his plan in a sudden but timely way. He radically restructured the nature of his business unit to include the control of fluid flow as well as the manufacturing of fluids, all of which was done to complement the production of the filter fibers. This led to the acquisition of several filter and valve manufacturers, and provided the necessary growth for his company. His plan was not as tightly thought out or voluminously detailed as those that commonly appear in planning documents. It couldn't be; rigidity of that kind would not have helped him adapt to changing circumstances.

How do effective managers use planning strategies? First, they use them as a guide for understanding what can be achieved in every personal encounter, even those that occur by chance. They ask themselves: Given what I'm trying to do, what information can I get from this person? What can I get this person to do for me? Second, these plans provide the backdrop for making even the most seemingly insignificant decisions. Managers should ask themselves: How does this decision contribute to my plan?

Obviously, not every such plan has the power and sweep of Mr. Sloan's. However, any manager can use his or her plan as a lever to nudge the organization, big or small, down the path to success. This is what good planning is all about. Some advice for good planning:

1) Discipline yourself to devote some time, regularly, to thinking about the direction in which the business is going. Ask yourself: What relevant events recently have become known, and how do these events change the way we do business? Doing so will keep your plan current.

2) Try to flesh out and develop the plan each time you think about it. The better developed the plan, the more powerful it is likely to be.

3) Use your plan daily. Ask yourself: Given what I'm trying to accomplish, what opportunities does this encounter

present? How can I use this decision to achieve my objectives?

Strategic-planning systems have the positive effect of forcing managers to think rigorously about the future of their businesses. However, the best planning is of a more informal kind. It takes place every day in managers' minds as they steer their organizations through changes in the business environment that cannot be foreseen.

Mr. Stengrevics is assistant professor of management policy at the Boston University School of Management.

Transform Leaden Strategies Into Golden Opportunities

By Kenichi Ohmae

It isn't fashionable to believe that planning is important to business success, especially for the Japanese. According to Western experts, Japanese managers don't plan; instead, they have an operational, factory-floor perspective, and their planning is little more than consensus building. The new management buzzwords are implementation and entrepreneurship.

Well, like so many management trends, this one, too, is an oversimplification. Japanese and Westerners both continue to use and need good strategic planning. Indeed, in most businesses the search for direction has never been so important. The difference now is that the nature of planning is changing, becoming more imaginative and demanding; compared with planning in the past, this new kind of strategy might be called "pre-planning."

During the 1970s, strategic planning started with a market forecast for a product—say, a widget. Planners pretty much accepted both the widget and its core customers and competitors as givens. Decisions were basically about how much, and when, to invest in making more widgets. Company after company spotted and pursued the same growth widget markets.

But today if you know which product to forecast for, then

you're already near the finish line. Planning today means determining which markets to pursue. Planners now have to grapple with a much fuzzier idea of a product or service, often something completely new.

There are several reasons for this: Technology now develops and matures much faster; competition has become global and tougher; many companies are diversifying beyond old markets, and consumer demand is growing more difficult to predict. For example: Should a company sell typewriters that include word processors? Should television be made part of stereo- and/or video-recording equipment or be continued on its own?

Consider Sony Corp.'s new portable compact disk player. The heart of it is an "everything" disk that can hold 500 to 1,000 times as much information as current floppy disks, plus graphics and digital audio. Clearly, Sony is entering the disk market, not just extending its Walkman product line. This makes a tremendous difference in strategic decisions concerning consumers, competitors and suppliers.

This problem of market definition is most extreme in fast-growing, high-tech industries, but it's also occurring in services. Take banking or consumer finance. Strategic planning now deals with the most basic decisions of the business—that is, what services to offer and to whom. Banks that are still planning only around traditional guideposts such as deposits are in trouble; they should be thinking about hundreds of other financial products.

Since the market definition is so difficult, demand forecasts may not be possible. A company may have to live with demand estimates that change as the market evolves. It's here that the implementers miss the point. Implementation is not just a matter of doing. Companies implement to learn as much as to do. They need to reassess their products as markets or technologies change, and that takes planning.

Sometimes that means reassessing the viability of the business itself. Brother of Japan looked at its main business, sewing machines, and realized that fewer and fewer Japanese women actually sew; they buy ready-made blouses. So Brother used its knowledge of precision machinery and microelectronics technology to diversify into office automation. It quickly became one of the world's biggest makers of electronic typewriters. Recar, another sewing-machine maker, planned only around its sewing machines, in which it had a healthy market share. It concentrated on perfecting its product without adapting to changes in the market. That market was collapsing, and earlier this year Recar went out of business.

Brother's new typewriter created a new market. It brought its sewing-machine accuracy to an existing product—typewriters—and changed the world's conception of that product. Traditional planning simply would have spotted the sewing-machine business as low-growth and recommended leaving it. Brother's "pre-planning" looked more carefully at fundamentals and strengths. Rather than looking for new markets to enter, this kind of planning imagines new markets to create.

In another example, Sumitomo Denko and Furakawa Denko, after examining their copper-wire businesses, decided to shift half to fiber optics. So despite the enormous differences between metallurgy and glass (which is used in fiber optics), both companies have diversified into optical wire.

Another new planning challenge is to recognize one's true competitors, because many new competitors will come from untraditional markets—often foreign or from a different industry. Seiko never expected Casio, which had focused on the hand-held calculators market, to be a serious competitor in its timepiece market. Instead, Seiko focused its competitive eye on the Swiss. However, when Casio applied its knowledge of electronics to the timepiece industry, it took off like a rocket in that market and has caused more headaches for Seiko than the Swiss ever could have caused.

Planners used to be able to "roll over" existing plans. But because those plans may contain faulty assumptions about markets, this practice becomes more dangerous all the time. Rolling over today means extending the risks. Planners now need to assess their markets and competitors without traditional assumptions. Otherwise they may get caught by surprise. And they need continuous information about customers and technology to know when to make changes.

Whether the original planners can do this new work adequately is an open question. But it's certainly true that planning has finally become truly strategic.

Mr. Ohmae is managing director of McKinsey & Co. in Tokyo. He is the author of "Triad Power" (Free Press, 1985).

Disorganized Like a Fox: The Sly Boss

By Jack Falvey

It's time some of the myths of time management were seriously challenged. Keeping time logs, handling each piece of paper only once and working from leather-bound time planners are all part of the folklore and old wives' tales of time management.

What's the sense of keeping a time log if the person you work for keeps you overloaded in the first place? Most people aren't allowed to manage their own time. When the phone rings they must answer it. They have no one to delegate to, and carefully negotiated objectives are added to continuously. Their only option is often to work almost around the clock or go elsewhere (which should be considered).

If you happen to be senior enough, or isolated enough, or blessed with a boss who gives you some operational breathing space, there are things you can do to increase the effective use of your time.

Begin, and never stop, spending a tremendous amount of your time looking for, hiring, and caring for the very best people possible. Time invested in that one area pays the greatest of all dividends.

One manager had a single subordinate and a secretary to run his department. While conducting interviews for the vacant secretarial position, he discovered a woman reentering the job market who had worked for senior management and was exceptionally talented. Not only did he hire her, but in a short period of time he entrusted her with approximately half of the day-to-day operations, and she ran them without a hitch. Each morning he brought her coffee and watered the plants. It was a small price to pay for more than doubling his discretionary time. After a year of heavy responsibility and flawless performance, she eventually built up the confidence she needed to seek her own management assignment.

Unfortunately most people were promoted into management because of hard work. They think that if long hours get them there, they should continue that practice in their managerial assignment. Trying to do everything is not management, it's addiction.

Adrenaline is a powerful drug. You can manufacture your own supply. Its overuse feels good. However, it was never intended for continued use and those who abuse it pay a great price. It is not necessary to sacrifice health and family to be successful, even if those around you believe that it is required.

Executive Henry Hamrock is a world-class time manager on a day-to-day basis, as well as in his overall career plan. When appointed vice president of sales at Mac-Bick, a medical-equipment company, he brought in from the field one of his brightest juniors and told him bluntly that it was his job to do the work. Not only did Henry often handle a piece of paper hundreds of times (because he could never find things on his desk), he arrived each day at 9 a.m. and departed promptly at 5 p.m. He carried a briefcase home with him, but it was just for effect; it never had anything in it. He concentrated on getting others to work hard for him. Few let him down. He kept no "to do" lists. He set few objectives. Everybody who worked for him worked like crazy just to keep him out of trouble.

Of course, Henry was disorganized like a fox. His subordinates felt that he couldn't get along without them. He listened to their ideas and tried many of them. Some didn't work very well, and he took full responsibility for the shortcomings and usually laughed them off. Because the company was small, Henry had a chance to buy some equity ownership. When the company was acquired, he retired in his early 50s to play golf full time between Palm Beach and Cape Cod.

Everyone said he would go crazy and soon return to action, but Henry marched to his own beat. He played golf and commuted spring and fall for 10 years, loving every minute of it. People finally believed that he was serious about his life of leisure.

When one of his sons came up with a new venture idea, Henry—now in his 60s—thought it looked good, put in start up funds, helped land some initial contracts, and became president of Aplicare, a supplier of clinical wipes. His friends all think he is crazy to begin a new business at his age. He just smiles and picks up the phone to see how sales are going for the month.

Your job is not to fill every waking moment with effort. Your job is to achieve results, and if you are a manager, that means through the efforts of others. Top priority becomes helping others achieve. You can't be sensitive to others if you are constantly busy.

For centuries military commanders have understood the principle of strategic reserves. Two units in the line with one in reserve. Time should be managed in much the same way. Everything worth doing should be accomplished in two-thirds of the time available with one-third held in reserve. A superior manager or commander will accomplish his or her objectives without employing the reserve. That's a far better strategy than 110% effort at all times. That kind of output must be the exception, not the rule.

How do you open up time? Try this. Cross several things off your "to do" list without doing them. It's almost magic how much time you can create with that method. See if you can figure out what you are best at. Do that and see if you can become even better at it.

Those workers and managers who think arriving early and working late is effective and productive should rethink their strategy. However, if you are a high-energy person who produces ideas around the clock, then get yourself a three-shift support staff. If you can't afford this, then why not work on one idea long enough so that it will produce enough return to indulge your output talent?

Now shut out the lights and go home; it's too late to be reading this article.

Mr. Falvey is a management consultant in Londonderry, N.H.

Superstars and Lone Rangers Rescue Dull Enterprises

By Rosabeth Moss Kanter

Executives reading inspirational accounts of outstanding corporations sometimes are bothered by the gap between the support for innovation and entrepreneurship attributed to the excellent companies and the lack of such support in their own environments. Managers attracted by the concept of innovation wonder how they ever could fit it into *their* companies. However, even in the most change-averse, control-conscious, innovation-discouraging companies, a few hardy souls still will take the initiative to innovate against the grain.

"Superstars" with strong track records and high credibility can innovate when others cannot. Even in unreceptive environments, a few superstars always have the power to do the extraordinary because of the force of their competence, the sponsorship of key executives or the awareness that they are being groomed for top slots. Indeed, the company relies on them for innovations. So they can bend rules, take daring steps and talk back to the big bosses. They are the ones who are given opportunities to get involved in designing products or systems. While everyone else is inhibited by an excessive hierarchy or the politics of turf protection, the superstars dash toward their goals.

Not everyone can be a superstar, of course, but there are

other outlets for entrepreneurship in innovation-discouraging companies.

"Rescue artists" (also known in some companies as "miracle workers") are brought in to turn around failing operations. Given a blank check to work on trouble spots, they often can bring in innovations that others are not permitted to make. For example, one aerospace company commonly gets most of its technical and manufacturing innovations in this manner. New contracts are run first by the usual division staff for a few years under tight constraints and equally tight budgets. A program manager's complaints that the project is in jeopardy receive no response other than exhortations to try harder. Then, as schedules start to slip and cost overruns build up, the program manager is abruptly replaced by a "rescue artist" for whom all previous constraints are removed. Freed temporarily of the handcuffs on his or her predecessor, creative work takes place. After the turnaround, the old rules are reapplied.

A third group of innovators can be dubbed "honeymooners." They are romanced by the company and brought in from outside with a change mandate—e.g., to start a new department. Expected to bring in fresh ideas and not expected to know the "rules" yet, they have a honeymoon period in which to innovate. One manager, hired to get an insurance company into modern marketing, used his position as an outsider to ask blunt, almost naive questions. He violated company protocol by hiring outside consultants, forming task forces, sharing the limelight with subordinates and getting staff members offices beyond their status. This enabled him to build an innovative marketing division and steal a march on the company's competitors.

"Creative opportunists" are able to capitalize on a "hole in the system"—a temporary chance to make changes because of new bosses or new budget cycles or a changeover of systems. At a local telephone operating company, where years of a solidifying bureaucracy had made innovation a rare, slow process, the few enterprising managers I saw were able to make use of resources for experiments during a reorganization. The few innovators at a bank I studied often were the beneficiaries of higher-level ignorance; they were able to go ahead with significant projects because their bosses either did not want to be bothered or were so remote they did not understand their subordinates' functions well enough to challenge the unusual requests in plans and budgets.

The last set of innovators-against-the-grain sometimes are called "Lone Rangers." They have a strong value orientation and are willing to battle the system for what they believe is right, even if they are alone in doing it. Outlaw as well as hero, these innovators may be ready to break minor rules to reach a greater goal. They may engage in sneaky budget transfers, using funds for a purpose only loosely related to the official one; hold off-site meetings to raise the morale of the troops even though the company frowns on such a practice; create their own reward systems; spend money before it is allocated, or even get a product on line before receiving official approval, as I saw an entrepreneurial engineering manager do at a leading manufacturing firm—thus netting a big financial gain.

Companies often derive great benefit from those willing to bootleg funds or disobey orders. One of the most important products in IBM's history, the 360 system, benefited from Lone Ranger actions. A research lab in San Jose, Calif., had been told explicitly to stop working on a low-power machine but continued anyway, despite top management's repeated orders. Ultimately, it turned out that the machine the lab had been working on solved a technical problem. It was incorporated into the line and reportedly sold better than any other in the series.

But there also are distinct drawbacks to the Lone Ranger innovation method. Lone Rangers may be wrongheaded as often as they are heroic. By barreling through the company's checkpoints and riding roughshod over usual procedures, they weaken the controls—including free and open discussion among colleagues—that screen out nonfeasible ideas. The goal should be to make companies *more* collaborative, not less so.

It also is unwise to depend upon Lone Rangers, or other

unusual innovators, for a company's innovations. Such un-guided entrepreneurial missiles can go off in all directions, undermining the coherent and integrated culture that is helpful for business excellence. Lone Ranger successes teach disrespect for leaders and cynicism about the formal system. By having rigid innovation-stifling rules and proce-dures, many companies force people to become "outlaws" in order to get anything done. But because this style some-times results in lucky breaks, the companies avoid taking a hard look at the appropriateness of their organization and practices.

The spirit of enterprise is alive and well in unexpected corners of unexpected companies. It certainly is encourag-ing to know that a few individuals with an entrepreneurial spirit may send out sprouts, even in otherwise uncongenial climates. Still, as encouraged as I am by sprouts, I would rather see whole gardens full of innovation.

Ms. Kanter is the author of "The Change Masters: Innova-tion for Productivity in the American Corporation," recently published by Simon & Schuster. She also is Professor of Management at Yale University and Chairman of Good-measure, Inc.

Hisao Tsubouchi, Japan's Mr. Turnaround

By Adam Meyerson

Hisao Tsubouchi fits few of the conventional images of Japanese businessmen. In a country that generally frowns on corporate takeovers, he has made a specialty out of acquiring bankrupt companies—usually at bargain-basement prices—and turning them around. Shunning the premium many of his countrymen put on seniority and elite education, he likes to give responsibility to young executives, and in hiring he says he "doesn't care if someone went to a good university." And while it's common for Japanese executives to boast of their mistresses, Mr. Tsubouchi takes pains to proclaim his fidelity to his wife, and says any manager who works for him and takes a "second wife" can forget about advancement.

Mr. Tsubouchi is also rich, unlike the salaried men who dominate Japanese industry. He and his wife are sole owners of a 160-company empire centered around the Kurushima Dockyard Co. on the southern island of Shikoku. The empire includes shipyards, steamship and ferry lines, food distributors, hotels, a bank and a newspaper, as well as valuable real estate such as a golf course. The companies are privately held, so public figures aren't available, but Mr. Tsubouchi says total sales are about $2.4 billion.

Mr. Tsubouchi is best known for his retrenchment and rescue of Sasebo Heavy Industries Co., a major shipyard that was about to go bankrupt in 1978 and which is now making money after a 60% cut in employment and a 40% cut in gross tonnage capacity. But apart from a chain of movie houses he acquired from his father, Mr. Tsubouchi obtained almost all of his 160 companies from the bankruptcy block.

On a recent evening at a hot springs resort he owns on Shikoku, Mr. Tsubouchi shared a dinner of raw lobster, seaweed and 17 other, mostly simple, dishes with a reporter and interpreter. He was reluctant to discuss in detail just how he turns around a failing company. He also begged off questions about his relations with the Japanese government, which exercises rather active administrative guidance over shipbuilding and shipping, and presumably plays some role in Mr. Tsubouchi's turnarounds. He spoke, however, of his general management principles, beginning with homage to the capabilities of ordinary workers.

"Sports records are broken every year," he says. "So if people work hard, they can break productivity records, too." He contends that productivity advances come much more from human effort and imagination than from capital investment. "The human being is much more efficient than any machine."

But workers often resist equipment or instructions that boost efficiency. To counteract this, says Mr. Tsubouchi, "When I groom managers, the most important thing I look for is how well they are trusted by blue-collar workers. If there is trust, then orders will be followed and labor relations will take care of themselves." To help win workers' trust, Mr. Tsubouchi says he insists that managers lead unextravagant lives and keep spartan expense accounts; that means, for example, few of the geisha parties so popular among most Japanese businessmen.

Executives should also be perceived to be doing their jobs as a "service to the company and its workers," not for personal gain. To strengthen this impression, whenever he takes over a bankrupt company, the managers he chooses receive no company salary until the enterprise breaks even. In the meantime, Mr. Tsubouchi says, he pays them personally.

Mr. Tsubouchi offers workers such common Japanese benefits as company housing and lifetime employment. In return for moderating wage demands, he says, he promises to keep a reserve enabling workers to feed their families even if business turns sour.

But he combines paternalism with a strict attention to cost-competitiveness, especially to slashing unit labor costs. He rejects the argument that comparative advantage in industries such as shipbuilding has shifted to lower-labor-cost countries such as Korea and Taiwan. "If wages in Korea are half as high as in Japan," he says, "that only means we have to be twice as productive." When he took over Sasebo, he argued that high labor costs were the major reason for its impending bankruptcy; in addition to slashing employment, he cut wages 15%, though he had to restore wage levels after a bitter two-month strike.

Mr. Tsubouchi's promise of lifetime employment is conditioned on willingness to be transferred, often suddenly, and to live if necessary in company dormitories. He boasts that he can shift 20% of one facility's work force to another on two weeks' notice.

He also likes to keep both management and technology simple. At Sasebo, he cut the managerial and technical staff from 460 to 37, and the number of work sections from 230 to eight; the result, he says, is that decisions could be made more quickly, because managers weren't getting in each other's way. He drastically cut the ship design department, choosing to cater to the low-cost segment of the market and arguing that the previous ships were too fancy and expensive to meet customers' needs.

He says he assigned the jobless ship designers to specific R&D projects, such as fuel-efficient engines and extraction of oil from tar sands. The engineers weren't to do R&D directly, but to canvass Japan for inventors whom Mr. Tsubouchi should finance and support. One result is the Nippon Clean Engine Laboratory Co., Tsubouchi-owned, which developed a low-pollution, quiet, fuel-efficient generator and heat pump, soon to be mass-produced by Kubota Engineering.

In addition to turning around companies, Mr. Tsubouchi devotes his energies to another kind of rehabilitation. Every year, in cooperation with the Public Prosecutor General's office, Kurushima Dockyard offers a training program for 60 to 70 convicts—including seven or eight murderers—who are serving the last year of their sentences. The prisoners live in a special dormitory but otherwise labor unguarded with other shipyard workers, and are taught such skills as welding and crane operation. One of the prisoners' responsibilities is to tend the doves that are released during christening ceremonies for Kurushima ships.

Nearly 1,700 prisoners have participated since the program was started in 1961. Mr. Tsubouchi says only five have escaped, while 15% have later been convicted of additional crimes. "My goal," says Mr. Tsubouchi, "is to give a second chance to both people and companies that everyone else considers a hopeless cause."

Mr. Meyerson is a former member of the Journal's editorial page staff.

5

Hiring and Firing

What You Can and Can't Learn From Interviews

By Martin H. Bauman

Many executives wonder how much they can really learn about a job candidate from a short interview. A face-to-face meeting is clearly helpful in judging a candidate's appearance, verbal skills and presence. But the applicant is typically on guard, dressed carefully and on his or her best behavior. Can you learn much about his personality and management style merely by talking with him?

Yes. A good interviewer can probe the candidate's basic mental and emotional patterns and determine whether he will fit not only the job but also the company. To do this, of course, it is absolutely essential to understand the requirements of the job and the "personality"—culture, traditions, style—of the company. Success in interviewing requires knowing what and whom you are looking for.

But don't reveal the professional background and personality traits needed for the job: Otherwise the applicant will give you the answers he thinks you want. Don't provide inadvertent clues by taking down answers which appear significant. A better technique would be to wait until the candidate is answering another question, and then write down the significant note.

One thing you will want to explore is your candidate's motivation: Does he seek power, for example, or achieve-

ment, or does he primarily need to be liked? Different moti-
vations will be appropriate for different kinds of assignments.

Helpful questions include: "What do you consider your
greatest accomplishment?" "Which job did you really enjoy
most and why?" "What do you enjoy doing in your leisure
time?" and, "What motivates you: money, power or achievement?"

An applicant who answers the last question with the
"money" response might inadvertently reveal something
quite different if he says his greatest accomplishment was
starting up a high-risk division within his company and
making it successful; his most pleasurable job one in which
there were daily crises; his greatest leisure time diversion
building fine wood cabinets. All of these are "achievement
answers" contradicting the candidate's own assessment of
himself.

Managerial Style: Certain positions require an executive
who has the ability to strongly motivate those around him,
to create a team. Other spots in the company, or other companies, need "the lone cowboy" type. Too often, however, an
interviewer will ask "What would you do if. . ." That's too
problematic or conditional, and an intelligent applicant can
probably tailor an answer to suit.

Better inquiries would be open-ended and based on past
performance. For instance, "How did you determine what
the people in your branch office were doing?"

One candidate might list daily phone calls, regular visits
and constant reports. Another will describe defining objectives and setting goals, while leaving the day-to-day details
to his staff. In the former case, we have a hands-on manager
who needs to be in control; in the latter we see someone who
prefers to operate at arm's length. Neither style is right nor
wrong, only appropriate or inappropriate for the job.

Values: One of the most revealing questions in this area is
"Tell me about the best boss and the worst boss you ever
had." While the worst boss answer can conjure up a picture
of the candidate's future superior—thus eliminating this
candidate—the "best boss" reply often indicates how the

applicant himself would like to be. For instance, he might say, "My best boss demanded results, but he was fair." The response suggests the interviewee's value system.

Personality: A set of interlocking questions, posed at different times, work well here. "Were you and your brother— or sister—alike when you were growing up?" "Are you and your wife—or husband—alike or different?" "What do you admire most in your spouse?"

Answers: 1) "We were very different. My brother was quiet and studious." 2) "We're very different. My wife is much more outgoing than I am." 3) "I admire my wife's ability to make friends easily."

The first two answers appear contradictory. They tell us of a boisterous youngster who became an introverted adult. But since people generally do not change that drastically, we must explore further. The third answer tells us something else: An applicant who, though still outgoing, is perhaps questioning his own ability to deal with people in social situations. (My wife is different. She makes friends easily.) Such a pattern of responses, though simplified here, suggests that this applicant might have difficulty if the job called for a great deal of socializing.

But just how much can you trust an individual's self-assessment? Most people do, in fact, know their strengths and weaknesses. They have been told them over and over again by superiors, family members and friends. But make sure the candidate's responses are consistent.

There are, of course, limitations to the face-to-face meeting, no matter how skilled the interviewer. Interviews cannot guarantee the detection of dishonesty, for those who possess that trait—along with alcoholism and paranoia—are notoriously clever at concealing it. Here an understanding of body language is useful. Eye aversion, hand-over-mouth, suddenly talking too fast or too hesitantly, a sudden flutter of the fingers, or anything that deviates from a pattern, could be meaningful, and is information that should be filed away.

Finally, there are some aspects of an applicant's life that are best learned elsewhere. In judging past performance, analytic skills and certain forms of intelligence, it's important to combine a careful interview with a battery of objective tests as well as extensive reference checks. These other sources of information also help guard the interviewer from the trap of "falling in love" with the candidate because of personal chemistry. However great that chemistry, love is often blind.

Mr. Bauman is president of Martin H. Bauman Assocs., a New York executive search firm.

What to Do When the Executive Recruiter Calls

By Frank R. Beaudine

Your phone rings and the call is from an executive recruiter. What should you do?

My advice is to listen carefully with an open mind to the search consultant's description of the position to be filled. If you're really not the slightest bit interested, say so gracefully. But if it sounds worth exploring, let your feelings be known. You don't lose points by expressing interest, provided you don't go overboard and try to overwhelm the recruiter with your credentials and capabilities.

Perhaps you feel uneasy talking at the office. If so, offer to call back or suggest another time when you can talk comfortably. Note of caution: Some search consultants are troubled by candidates who insist that they can be called only at home. It conveys a feeling of insecurity.

Or perhaps you've never heard of the search firm or have qualms about the caller. Usually a consultant will try to establish credibility at the outset by mentioning mutual friends or business acquaintances, some of whom may have suggested you. You can also check a firm's reputation through business friends or other search consultants you may know personally. It is perfectly legitimate to ask the caller how long the firm has been in business, what kinds of companies it serves and whether it is national or regional.

If you're the super-cautious type, you may wish to ask for references.

Depending on your level of achievement, the search consultant probably already knows a great deal about your work record and education. More often than not he has already determined that you have the experience and skills his client needs.

But the consultant doesn't know whether your personal chemistry will be compatible with the client's. That, together with details related to your technical qualifications, he would want to explore in a personal interview. The consultant's primary purpose in calling is to determine whether an interview is justified. He must determine whether under a given set of circumstances you are willing to move.

The search firm assumes that you are satisfied with your present position. Indeed, at least 95% of candidates approached are happy and doing well in their work.

The consultant will try to determine during your phone conversation whether the position he is seeking to fill could offer you attractive opportunities in terms of responsibility, title, income, location and career growth potential. It is along these lines that his questions will proceed without much attempt at getting deeply into specifics.

You will understandably be reticent to discuss such matters in an initial phone conversation; the recruiter understands that confidentiality is as important to you as to his client. To arrive at an interview decision, however, he needs certain information. If the position sounds appealing, you should respond as forthrightly as possible.

In turn, you should ask your own questions. One you shouldn't ask is the name of the company involved. At this stage, client confidentiality must be protected. You can expect, however, to be told in general terms the industry it is in, its size and where the post is located. Apart from the title of the position, you will want to know its reporting relationships as well as why the company isn't promoting from within. The general parameters of income are appropriate for discussion.

Be frank about any reservations you have, about either the position or personal difficulties you would face in making a move. This could involve relocation and/or family considerations, which may be negotiable. If you are reluctant, it is better to express this before a personal interview is arranged. A professional recruiter will respect your decision.

Guard against one who tries to sell you on the position. A seasoned consultant recognizes that it is neither in your nor his client's interest to try to persuade a candidate who is less than enthusiastic. His role is to present a career opportunity, not to act as a sales agent.

Bear in mind that although recruiters are paid only by a client company, never by a candidate, they are not unmindful of the importance of satisfying both parties. Incompatibility or dissatisfaction on either part would be counterproductive. As a consequence, the responsible consultant will be as concerned for the candidate as for the client, so don't feel hurt if you are told the position is not right for you. It is not a reflection on your abilities.

Assuming the consultant decides to pursue you as a candidate, and you agree to throw your hat in the ring, I have one last admonition. Be patient. Most searches involve about three months. A very senior position can take longer. Don't try to accelerate the process; that usually backfires.

Mr. Beaudine is chairman of Eastman & Beaudine Inc., an international search firm headquartered in Chicago.

Advice for Job Seekers
By Robert M. Hochheiser

Whether you are out of work or just looking for a better paying opportunity, there is no such thing as a foolproof way to get hired. You can, however, boost your chances if you are willing to work hard at aggressively promoting yourself. Here are some guidelines.

Get your foot in the door. In contacting a prospective boss for the first time, your sole objective is to get an interview. If you expect to get hired before the employer has "seen the merchandise," you are in for a heavy disappointment.

The only reason for sending in a resume or application letter is therefore to motivate an employer to meet with you. And that means you shouldn't say anything in a letter or resume that has even the slightest chance of keeping you off his already overcrowded interview schedule. If you think the boss wants an MBA and you didn't even go to college, don't mention your education. Show that you are good at what you do and that you meet whichever criteria you know about, but if you don't meet a given requirement, don't give evidence that shows you to fall short.

Does this mean that you should lie? No, it only means that you shouldn't volunteer information that might be considered in a negative light. Such information can be deadly prior to an interview, but may not hurt at all when divulged *after* you have had a chance to make a good impression in person.

Don't apply for a job unless you can make a case for doing it well. If you can make such a case, whet the employer's appetite for wanting to meet you: Be specific, focus on how good you are and don't say anything that might be viewed as a negative. Most important, ask for an interview; you can't get a hit unless you first get up to bat.

Apply in quantity. Oil people know that to get a gusher, they may have to drill a lot of holes. As a job-seeker, you must operate the same way. To get a good offer for a good job, you must be prepared to apply—one at a time—to an army of potential employers.

Aside from going after every advertised job appropriate to your field, make yourself known to recruiters and employment agencies. Apply to every employer whose needs you could make a strong case for meeting.

If you are sending fewer than several dozen applications every week, you're not trying hard enough. For if you don't make the contacts, someone else will.

Tailor your sales pitch to the reader. With the exception of companies looking for a trainee or a corporate president, few employers will be interested in a well-rounded jack-of-all-trades. Usually, prospective bosses will be impressed only if your skills, achievements, educational background and experience are first rate and directly applicable to the specific job they want done as well as to their specific business. They don't care about anything else. When you include, in a resume or letter, information that is not pertinent, you waste space that you could otherwise use to focus on job-related strengths. You also waste the reader's time, an accomplishment that never makes a good impression.

So tailor your application as closely as possible to the known or probable requirements of the job you seek. That may be difficult when you are sending out hundreds of applications. At the least, segregate your targets into groups having similar interests and pursue each group on a tailored basis. Even with individualized cover letters, however, a resume covering your entire career isn't tailored to anything and may point up negatives rather than focusing on your strengths. You'll do a lot better if you throw away your resume and use a series of well-written letters, each of which is customized to highlighting your strengths relative to a specific set of hiring requirements, and whenever possible, personally addressed to whomever you would report if hired.

Don't promise to deliver more than the employer requires. If employers want more, they'll ask for it. Should you offer too much or your claims be too extravagant, you may be viewed as either a dreamer or someone prone to incur significant risks in pursuit of unrealistic goals. Similarly, if you look too good on paper, the reader may erroneously conclude that your salary requirements are too high or that you would be unlikely to be satisfied with the job for long.

They may be right. Perhaps the job is not a good one for you. But why prejudge? Don't oversell, get your foot in the door and decide for yourself.

Ask questions before you give answers. When you get a telephone or in-person interview, don't make the mistake of allowing yourself to just sit there and be interrogated. Take control of the interview by asking questions. Find out what the employer wants. Then use the answers as clues about which of your skills, experiences and accomplishments to emphasize.

Before the interviewer starts grilling you, ask him to describe what has to be done on the job you are discussing. When you hear something that coincides with one of your strengths, pounce on it and talk about your abilities in that area. Then, probe for details about on-the-job challenges you might encounter. Again, you'll get answers that will clue you in on what to talk about.

When a question comes your way, answer it directly and honestly, but always in a way that puts you in the best light. Answer only the question that has been asked of you; don't ramble on, don't go off to another subject and don't volunteer negatives. If you don't understand a question, request a clarification. Similarly, should a question seem too general, ask for it to be restated in a more specific manner.

In asking and answering questions, don't hog the conversation and don't be argumentative. Give the impression that you are an intelligent, competent professional who can get the job done and who is genuinely interested in finding out about it.

Keep at it. The foregoing requires an enormous amount of effort and you may not strike a gusher overnight. If your goals are realistic, however, don't let up. Jobs invariably go to those who do the best job of creatively "selling" their services to employers, and proper implementation of these steps can provide the edge that motivates an employer to interview and hire *you* rather than someone else.

Mr. Hochheiser, a Monsey, N.Y., outplacement consultant, is author of "Throw Away Your Resume" (Barron's Educational Series).

The Agonizing Decision of Cutting Corporate Staff

By Carol Hymowitz

I'm sorry but we don't have a job for you here anymore.
It's the toughest thing a manager ever has to say to an employee.

Weyerhaeuser Co., the Seattle-based forest products concern that was hurt by the slump in housing, was undergoing its biggest staff cutback ever. President and Chief Executive Officer George Weyerhaeuser ordered the reductions in an effort to pare overhead and improve productivity. To survive in the "turbulent" business climate of the 1980s, he told his senior executive staff, "We're all going to have to work toward a leaner, flatter organization." More than 800 of Weyerhaeuser's salaried employees, 6% of corporate staff, had been let go and more reductions were planned.

The department-level managers who had to make the cuts weren't issued any specific number targets. Instead, they were being told to focus first on eliminating positions, rather than people, and to "redesign" their departments as if they were organizing their own businesses. "We're asking managers, 'How would you arrange jobs if this was your own company and you wanted the best productivity, the best return?'" said Frank Guthrie, a member of one of three "organization redesign" committees that were helping to oversee the staff cuts. (There were 10 members on Mr.

Guthrie's committee.) "We're asking, 'Which jobs are absolutely essential and which can go?'"

The answers vary. Weyerhaeuser's largest forest-products division, in Longview, Wash., cut 134 positions, or 26% of its salaried staff, by merging two accounting groups and combining the sales and distribution of lumber, panel and consumer products into a single department. Managers of the corporate engineering department met for more than two months before deciding to eliminate one level of management. This and other steps cut almost 100 jobs, one-third of the department.

Department managers then had to undertake the more difficult task of choosing who would fill the reduced number of jobs. Top performers with essential skills or, better yet, the ability to do more than one job were obvious choices. But there were many gray areas—whether, for example, to keep a "superperformer" who had problems working in a team (he was laid off) or what to do with managers whose jobs had been eliminated. "We decided it was better to let them go than bump them down to a job level they were overqualified for," said Mr. Guthrie. Those with 20 years or more seniority, however, were guaranteed a job somewhere in the company.

Mr. Guthrie believed it was important to be direct in breaking the news. "We've been guilty at times when dealing with marginal performers of hiding behind the 'organization redesign' facade," he said. "But people really want to know why me. We've learned that we have to give a reason."

However, many may be too shocked to listen. "A lot of times after they hear they're being let go, they don't hear anything else," said Mr. Guthrie. Indeed, although he always explained the generous severance package Weyerhaeuser was offering—dismissed employees could remain on the payroll for up to five months, then receive a week of severance pay for each year of service and also get free counseling from an outplacement center—most people didn't pay full attention. So the terms were offered in writing as well and another time was scheduled to discuss them.

Executives at other companies agree that the selection

process involves agonizing choices. A manager at a major oil company who didn't want to be identified worries about whether he will have to drop his closest colleague, "someone I use as a sounding board but who doesn't produce much himself. If I'm really pressed for bodies I'm not going to be able to justify keeping him." An executive at Westinghouse Electric Corp., guilty about having to eliminate anyone, fires "the guy who has the better chance of getting another job."

The hardest part, most executives agree, is breaking the news. "You can't help but identify with the person you're telling and you always have to wonder if somehow you failed him as a supervisor," says the oil company manager.

Some put off breaking the news for so long that "when they finally do it they're so guilty and angry they explode and heap insults on the poor person," says Robert Swaine, president of Eaton Swaine Associates Inc., an outplacement company in New York. Mr. Swaine believes a "termination discussion should be a monologue not a dialogue," and he advises managers to keep the discussion short and "talk about the position not the person. Don't say, 'You're fired.' Say, 'We've come to a decision about your position.'"

Mr. Swaine also thinks people should be fired in the morning, preferably in the middle of the week and certainly not at 4:55 p.m. on a Friday "when you'll just be sending them home to a lonely, desperate weekend. If you fire people in the middle of the week, you can send them to an outplacement firm to get help writing a new resume."

A growing number of companies, perhaps hoping to avoid "subjective" firings, are instituting voluntary resignation programs. Xerox Corp., for example, accepted resignations from 160 employees in its product development and engineering operations in Rochester, N.Y. As a result, it was able to cut by more than 50% the number of dismissals it had planned in their departments.

Of course, companies using voluntary resignation risk losing their best and most needed people. Thus, at Xerox, managers could choose not to offer the program in their departments.

Managers say they should be prepared to listen to those they fire and even admit that maybe they made a mistake. "One guy who was being sent off to outplacement argued that the service he'd been offering a client couldn't be provided by anyone else," says Weyerhaeuser's Mr. Guthrie. "We looked into it and he was right, so we renegotiated a job with him." When you're making decisions about whether people keep their jobs or not, "you better know that you are going to make some mistakes."

Carol Hymowitz is a member of the Journal's Pittsburgh bureau.

Hiring a Teen-ager for the Summer

By Frank J. Macchiarola

Every year, thousands of businesses are bombarded by appeals from organizations like mine. We ask businesses to provide summer jobs for disadvantaged teen-agers because we think it is important to introduce these youngsters to the world of work. We believe that their preparation for work requires some contact with adults at a worksite. We believe it's not charity, it's just good business.

Employers vary in their response. Some have openings that need to be filled, whether because of rapid turnover or because of staff vacations. Some see it as a challenge and responsibility to teach the rules of the workplace to youngsters who may never have been exposed to them. Others don't like the way many teen-agers dress or behave, and fear that hiring them would be more trouble than it's worth. Most teen-agers can make productive summer employees if employers are prepared to do the following things:

Make certain the job is meaningful. An employer owes it to the youngster—and himself—to provide a real job. "Busy work" is a nuisance for the manager who has to supervise it, and it really is no service to the summer employee. Indeed, the most valuable thing a business can provide a teen-ager is the sense that he can do an important job that other people want done and are willing to pay for.

Examples of summer jobs held by teenagers are wide-ranging, from the esoteric (such as assistant keeper at the Bronx Zoo or packing pickles at the B&G Pickle Works in Queens) to the predictable (fast-food worker at a McDonald's franchise or service clerk handling trouble calls at New York Telephone).

Explain the most fundamental rules of the workplace. Rules and procedures that are routine to your other employees will be completely new to many summer hires. The youngster may not know how important it is to be on time or to be properly dressed. Schools aren't always the best teachers of what to expect in the workplace. Punctuality, attendance, dress standards and relationships with supervisors and co-workers must be explained and emphasized over and over. The young employee should also know exactly what his benefits are, what the payroll procedures are and what the procedure is in case of a grievance.

One good way to emphasize the importance of proper dress and punctuality is to point out that any business operation is a team effort and depends on teamwork just as competitive sports do. If a member of the team is late for work or isn't dressed right for the game, the whole team's performance suffers. If the team is working in an office, slacks, shirt and tie for men and skirt and blouse for women are most likely to gain acceptance for the young person among co-workers. If the job is a "dirty" one, work clothes can nevertheless be neat and orderly.

Evaluate performance. Summer hires are really no different from regular full-time employees when it comes to job evaluations. They will perform better if they know what is expected of them, and if they understand the criteria against which their performance will be judged. Evaluations should also provide feedback to the youngster on how he might improve his skills.

Be prepared to fire the youngster who breaks the rules. Other workers are looking to see if you carry out the rules as you say you will. They are used to discipline on the job, so it is important for young summer employees to understand that the same standards apply to them. Otherwise morale will break down. Most youngsters would rather live by adult standards when working with adults, rather than by any special rules of their own.

Employers and employees alike have often been enthusiastic about summer job programs. The teen-agers gain work experience that serves them well in the future. They learn what it is like to work with adults as well as what is expected of them in the world outside school. They gain self-confidence or vocational training for permanent jobs after school or college. And for thousands of businesses, they do jobs that need to be done.

Mr. Macchiarola is president of the New York City Partnership Inc., a private, non-profit organization of business and civic leaders. Formerly he was chancellor of the New York City school system.

Bringing Retired Talent Back to the Fore

By Phillip Shatz

For the past five years I have had the privilege of working with a once-retired lawyer who is now 77 years old, a former name partner in a prestigious New York law firm. He had been retired for about five years when he approached me about his assisting me. He conceded that he had lost interest in life and thought that if he got involved in the law again, he would regain a sense of participation in life.

Today, John has lost 40 pounds and shed 40 years. He is as aggressive and hard-driving as any of the 11 lawyers in our firm. His legal skills, honed by some 50 years' experience, make him our guru—the source of good judgment, novel legal concepts, encouragement and a perspective we would lack but for him.

John deals with clients, explaining, encouraging and counseling them in ways that constantly teach me. His professional skill is respected and admired by judges and lawyers alike. He writes briefs, draws contracts, researches, attends conferences and does everything without concession to his age, except perhaps that he works only about seven hours a day. When there is a crisis, he has been known to put in 17-hour days like the rest of us.

On reflection, I noted that in my past experience there had been three other senior executives who had contributed to the success of enterprises for which I was responsible.

Some years ago, my then law partner and I came into control of a savings and loan association. My role as president and chief executive officer was a part-time position and subordinate to our law practice. We decided that the opportunity existed to expand the bank and to open branches.

Our advertisement for a branch manager brought a response from a gentleman who did not mention his age but said he had been the secretary of the Federal Reserve Board of New York when he retired. After retirement, he had been appointed conservator of a large, financially troubled savings bank and had just completed a position acting as consultant to a major New England bank, writing an operating manual for its branch managers.

For branch manager, I had had in mind a person in the early 20s, with salary a small fraction of what Walter had been earning. I called Walter to thank him for his letter and to explain that he was over-qualified for the job. I told him that we would not be able to pay him a salary commensurate with his skills and that he might find the work tedious. Walter persuaded me to have lunch with him and proceeded to sell himself. He was financially secure but bored, and, as he put it, "How many times can I paint my house?" Walter found us at age 73. Failing eyesight forced him to resign at age 81; until then, we had benefited greatly from his expertise and skill, which played a large part in our fivefold growth while he was with us.

During those years, I was also chairman of an insurance firm. The company was plagued by lack of financial controls. A friend of mine, a minister, told me of a former bank vice president who was retired but was seeking work. Alex organized, and for over 10 years oversaw, the finances of that insurance company, with a resultant growth of sales and profits. He always said the work kept him alive and young. When Alex was 70, he asked if I would meet an older friend of his who he felt could contribute to the insurance firm. The result was a five-year experience with a man whose vitality belied his 80-year age. Harold was perhaps the youngest in perspective of these fine men. He was charming, urbane, knowledgeable about insurance and a great motivator of men.

In each of these cases, a very successful, bright and useful member of the business community had been deprived of the opportunity to contribute, and society was deprived of his knowledge and experience. In each case, compensation was irrelevant. They all expressed the view that they would work for nothing if only allowed to work. For them, the frustration of inaction was a destructive force, not only in their own lives but in those of their families.

I am aware of the corps of retired executives organized by the Small Business Administration, offering consulting services free of charge to any business that will ask. In my view, this program has several weaknesses.

The thrust of the corps is toward the business in trouble. The seniors I have met would prefer to apply their skills to ongoing and growing enterprises where they are likely to see fruitful results for their labors. Also, the emphasis on consultation precludes the satisfaction of being a permanent part of an organization, an integral part of the rewards these men seek. I believe political considerations would inhibit government support of the placement of retirees in permanent positions, given the current state of unemployment.

Moreover, the SBA does not have facilities in smaller communities where trained managers are in more limited supply and where retirees and small businesses exist in large numbers.

Can a marketplace be created where the skills of seniors can be matched with employers' needs? I believe the solution is not creation of a marketing vehicle but encouragement for each sector to seek the other. In every one of the experiences I have related, the senior said, "Let me start at no salary and let's determine compensation after you see what I am worth." What an irresistible argument. This offer should open most doors. As the skills show themselves and the results become apparent, my experience has been that the compensation offered uniformly exceeds the expectations or desires of the senior. On the other side, what ambitious retiree can resist the request from a business of "Will you help me?" An appeal to these proud and able men and women to use their skills will bring them charging to work with enthusiasm and verve, bringing with them their decades of experience.

My advice is for each segment to prospect. Look in your church, your club, and among your customers and people with whom you deal. Seniors, sell yourselves. Companies, sell your needs.

Mr. Shatz is a partner in the Poughkeepsie, N.Y., law firm of McCabe & Mack.

No Room for Loyalty

By Harvey Gittler

Dear Dave,

I've been mulling over something you said about feeling hurt because you were fired (I don't like the euphemism laid off) after 20 years of being a loyal employee.

Loyalty, Dave, is not the correct term to describe the relationship between an employee and an employer in an industrial or business organization. When was it that your company asked you to take a loyalty oath? When was it that your company pledged loyalty to you? I think you're confusing terms: integrity, honesty, compassion are noble attributes that you have every right to expect from your employer, but they do not constitute loyalty.

The dictionary defines loyal or loyalty as "faithful in allegiance to one's lawful sovereign or government; faithful to a private person to whom fidelity is due; faithful to a cause, ideal, or custom." Your company or my company or any other company is not a sovereign or a government. Nor is the company a person, a cause, an ideal, or a custom.

You and I go to work each day, and we are expected to put forth our best efforts and use our talents to their fullest. Perhaps we are even expected to give service above and beyond the call of duty, or at least above and beyond what we are being paid for at the moment. In turn, we expect to be paid a fair wage or an agreed-upon wage. And our service is compensated on a weekly, biweekly or monthly basis. That is where loyalty begins and ends; we give our service, and the company pays us for that service.

We can be expected to perform to the limits of our ability, to act in a concerted or team effort, to give the added measure—but for reasons other than loyalty. And we can expect our employer to show fairness, decency and even compassion—but for reasons other than loyalty.

When any employee works throughout a weekend to repair a machine so the factory can operate the next day, it is not an act of loyalty to the company. When an individual or group of individuals works long and arduous hours to make a presentation to a prospective client, it is not an act of loyalty to the company. When a lawyer works nights and weekends to complete a brief, it is not an act of loyalty to the firm. All of these are acts of loyalty to ourselves, to the individual making the sacrifice.

People work hard and extend themselves because they expect something in return. They expect to be paid for their efforts and eventually expect promotions, bonuses, or perhaps only a pat on the back. No one can expect more.

I would not be disloyal to my employer if I did not do the best job I know I am capable of doing. I would be disloyal to myself. And if a company kept an employee on, in spite of his doing a mediocre job, because he or she has 20 or 30 years of service, and said it was being done out of loyalty to the employee, then the company would be disloyal to other employees, to its stockholders, and to itself.

Remember when the two of us worked along with Ed What's-His-Name as senior engineers on that project? Remember that Ed, who had been with the company 10 years longer than we had, was getting about 10% more than we were? You and I asked each other why all three of us weren't getting the same salary since we were doing the same work. We questioned the fairness of the seniority system that resulted in Ed's higher rate of pay. We never did resolve that question of fairness, but you and I both ended up with better jobs than Ed. So in the long run, what did Ed's loyalty to the company entitle him to?

Loyalty is not something to give or to expect. Loyalty is an act each person gives or shows to himself. When an employee says that he or she has been loyal to the company, what that really means is, "I haven't changed jobs or sought employment elsewhere. I have (without being asked) devoted my time to this organization." And what is being asked in return is not to be fired, not to be let go, not to be part of a cutback. But were these facts part of the original hiring agreement? Did the company ever say that in return for years of service, the company would keep the employee on until retirement?

The Wall Street Journal once reported that a 12-year veteran with a soft-drink company was leaving to become the executive vice president of a competing soft-drink company. Was Mr. X disloyal to his company by leaving it for a better job? Was I disloyal to our employer when, 10 years ago, I left? And were you loyal because you stayed on for another 10 years? Would someone in that company who has been there 40 years, to your 20, be twice as loyal as you?

Any new company starting up and growing must, by your definition, be made up of employees who were disloyal to their last employer. After all, they left their previous employer to go to work for the new company.

Over the past 34 years, I have had several employers, and I would like to think that I gave to each above and beyond the call of duty. But I was acting out of loyalty to myself. I was striving for advancement, for rewards, and for the security that comes only from being of value to my employer. I have left companies to take new jobs that seemed to promise advancement—responsibility and money—but not out of an act of disloyalty to my employer. It was more out of an act of loyalty to myself, to my cause, to my ideals.

None of this is to say that long service should not be recognized and/or protected. But that recognition and/or protection should come out of corporate policy and practice, and an employee should know just what the policies and practices of the organization are. Such policies and practices should not be kept a secret. From my vantage point, compassion and understanding usually are not a part of the human resources development program. (The term human, in industry, does not imply humane. Human is a term used to distinguish people from machines or material.)

You will find another job, Dave. And you will succeed. But remember this time, all you owe to your employer is honesty, integrity and compassion.

Best regards,
Harvey

Mr. Gittler is materials manager for a heating and air-conditioning manufacturer. He was vice president for a medical-instrument company when he was fired at the age of 60. He does not consider his being fired an act of disloyalty, but rather an act of stupidity.

Your Right to Fire and Its Limits

By Thomas R. Horton

The trend away from termination at will should concern all employers, as it represents an increase in government intrusion—never a savory prospect. But much of that intrusion has been invited by poor management practices with regard to human resources.

A 1959 lawsuit set the precedent for all the at-will cases that followed. *Petermann vs. International Brotherhood of Teamsters* was initiated by an employee who was fired because he refused to perjure himself for his employer before an investigative legislative body.

"It would be obnoxious to the interests of the state and contrary to public policy and sound morality," said the California Appeals Court, "to allow an employer to discharge any employee. . . on the ground that the employee declined to commit perjury."

Since then, courts in various parts of the country have used this precedent to rule in favor of employees who have been fired for upholding a "public policy" issue. In *Nees vs. Hock,* a state court affirmed a jury award of compensatory damages to an employee fired for serving on a jury, finding that the employee had been discharged based on "such a socially undesirable motive that the employer must respond in damages for any injury done."

In still another instance, a court ruled in favor of an employee who had been fired for refusing to participate in an illegal price-fixing scheme. The court said that an employer's authority over its employee does not include the right to demand that the employee commit a criminal act to further its interests.

Clearly, on the basis of these and many other cases, we threaten our freedom through our own poor management. How can employers make bold claims about their employees being their greatest resource, and at the same time ask those employees to subvert their civic and moral natures? Yet, even now, some companies continue to act in a self-destructive fashion.

Such companies are resorting to surprisingly negative tactics in response to their fear of at-will legal challenges. In the application forms prospective employees must sign, some employers now explicitly state their right to terminate at will. These employers are beginning to compile employees' dossiers before they have even started work. The implication is that these employers don't have great confidence in their ability to manage people well.

An employee at my company told me that he once was interviewed for a job elsewhere, and was interested in taking the position until he saw just such a statement on the application form. He said: "That was the end of the interview; there was no way I was going to sign that document. I was offended, but beyond that it seemed to me that this company just didn't have its act together."

Nevertheless, in a recent article published by the Alexander Hamilton Institute, attorney Kenneth McCulloch advises companies to "make your application form into an 'acknowledgement of waiver' form." He suggests including the following boilerplate: "I agree to conform to the rules and regulations of the company and acknowledge that these rules and regulations may be changed, interpreted, withdrawn or added to by your company at any time, at the company's sole option and without any prior notice to me. I further acknowledge that my employment may be terminated, and any offer of employment, if such is made, may be withdrawn, with or without cause, and with or without prior notice, at any time, at the option of the company or myself."

This attorney also advises including a "reservation of rights" provision in the organization's personnel documents. The language he suggests is similar to the "acknowledgement of waiver" form, again asserting the organization's right to change the rules of the game however and whenever it pleases, along with its right to fire. And, in fact, some companies now do include right-to-terminate statements in their employee handbooks.

In our pre-occupation with our right as employers, we are unwittingly sending out the wrong message—that is, we are emphasizing our freedom to fire people for no good reason. Worse yet, abuse of our current freedom, in light of our recent legal history, may result in more—not less—government intrusion into business affairs.

A lawyer I know who advises employers on employment-at-will cases disagrees radically with the attorney whose article I quoted from. In fact, he believes that right-to-fire statements in application forms and in employee manuals may be found illegal in the courts, and could in themselves generate lawsuits.

In West Germany, the law against unjust dismissal protects the employee rather than the employer. Although it doesn't prevent employers from firing for just cause, it has effectively created a corporate culture that avoids termination. A manager from a major German chemical company told me he envied the freedom of American companies to fire incompetents. He said, "You wouldn't believe some of the deadwood we support." I asked him if it was impossible to be fired at his company, and he replied: "If you spit directly into the eye of the director general, he might fire you; or, he might just say that it was raining!"

We should allow neither the government nor lawyers to dictate how we treat our people. The way we treat our people, within legal limits, should be our prime concern. If the specter of legislation disturbs us, then our senior managers must ensure that our companies behave responsibly so that we will be able to retain control over termination.

An organization must have the right to fire incompetent personnel. Indeed, it has the obligation to its stockholders to do so. It must have the right to reduce its work force in hard times, if that is what it needs to do to survive. But the organization behaves self-destructively when it tells its employees that it values the right to treat them capriciously.

———————

Mr. Horton is president and chief executive of American Management Associations, a New York-based consulting firm.

Hitting Rock Bottom After Making It to the Top

By James F. Turner

I am far more cognizant now of TV commercials and ads in the The Wall Street Journal, as well as articles in various magazines, about acute emotional depression. The unanswered questions of how and why it happened to me continue to circulate in my mind.

As a "Type A" personality I felt mentally indestructible. After all, I had been a champion wrestler, a fearless naval aviator landing jets on carriers at night, and a businessman who solved hairy problems and took risks in stride. How can a fearless one fear?

Executives and managers, especially those high on the organizational chart, are particularly vulnerable to depression; higher equates with lonelier. Self-protection dictates one can't unburden one's emotional weakness with subordinates or competitive peers—or anyone else for that matter. The ultimate in emotional isolation is the chief executive. He can display no weakness, admit to no doubt or fear, and few, if any, subordinates would dare broach the subject of his mental well-being with him.

With the genius of hindsight, I can track all the symptoms of the past two years that led to my removal as chief executive officer of my company, and the reduction of function in my brain and personality. But the fear that accompanies depression is insidious. It creeps up on you. Not aware that I was already in the grip of a depression, I felt something was wrong.

I had a long-overdue physical, but found nothing abnormal for a healthy 48-year-old—eyes checked OK; cut down on smoking; began to walk regularly with my wife. I also began to do less and brood more, excusing the brooding by calling it contingency planning. Business had been bad during the recent recession, but there were positive signals that we would make it. However, I saw no signals, only black gloom and doom. I began to fear things that I had never feared before—my employees, the telephone, mail. I felt there was no one I could talk to about my fears. My wife and immediate subordinates sensed something was wrong, but they too knew not what.

If only someone, including myself, had recognized the symptoms and taken a firm hand. If I had taken a mental "physical" prior to taking a nose dive. If only I had someone—anyone—to talk to about the inane fears that began to get bigger and bigger until they conquered.

The true hell of a depression is the absolute negative outlook on every phase of life—the never-ending series of compartments that are all black, the certitude that nothing will turn out right—and the awful conclusion that since everything is black and forever will be, there is no point in life. Physically OK, one loses aggressiveness, pleasure, creativity, humor, inquisitiveness, concentration, interest, initiative and impatience—the last the only positive note.

My own depression, much like the tropical kind that grows into a hurricane, began to increase in intensity in the last couple of months. Looking back, I can even see a distinct change in my signature. There had been a gradual but accelerating change in relation to my associates and subordinates, characterized by my withdrawal. I began to feel that all communications, regardless of content, were negative, and through association, turned these feelings toward the bearer. Peer contacts, generally lunches with CEOs of other companies, which I enjoyed at least twice monthly, trickled to a halt. As I withdrew further I became reluctant to call the necessary management meetings.

I also had many of the classic physical symptoms of depression—dry mouth (constantly needed tea or water), chest pain, racing heart, hot flashes and that awful cold lead ball in the stomach. I was pointed straight down at close to terminal velocity.

My wife saved me in the nick of time, no doubt galvanized by reading my plans for my memorial service that I had (intentionally?) left on my bureau. A frantic call to our physician, and a quick trip to a psychiatrist, and the situation temporarily froze into a confused hiatus. At this point I could not see or face anyone except my immediate family, could not answer the telephone and was a classic nervous wreck. Past, present and future were painted in shades of blue-black.

The analogy of weather depression and human depression seems to me a good one. Just as a tropical depression can dissipate into a mild rainstorm, so can the temporary blues. However, some tropical depressions build into hurricanes, and those depressive blues can escalate into a human swirl of treacherous pessimism that renders one incapable of sound judgment at the least, and the unthinkable at worst.

With the help of my wife, psychiatrist and a couple of books, I began to investigate how and what had happened, and tentatively began to explore what lay in the future. I now know what happened—acute depression rendering me incapable of sound judgment. I still do not know why. I do know that what happened was preventable, and that it is curable.

The painful lessons I have learned may help someone. It may be you. It may be an associate, friend or relative. Be aware that depression is real. It can hit anyone, and I mean anyone. I strongly suspect that most victims of depression do not recognize their own vulnerability until it is too late. One of the most cogent warning signals is the drift toward the inability to enjoy, particularly things that previously were pleasurable. If you have any doubts about yourself, perhaps a conversation with a professional about feelings and fears, without the risk of exposure, would be in order.

I am creeping back into the world now. I answer a telephone occasionally, although during bad periods I take it off the hook. I make lists and follow through, although the physical items are far easier to accomplish than the mental ones, such as writing this article.

There is no time frame for cure and recovery. My reservoir of adaptive energy was drained; although it's still low, it is now no longer leaking. With my wife, God, professional help and friends I am putting my life back together, never to be the same. But perhaps, just perhaps, it will be a little better.

Mr. Turner is a former chief executive officer who lives in Baltimore, Md.

Questions to Ask
When You're Fired

By Robert Coulson

What can you do when you learn that you are about to lose your job?

It is a mistake to accept your termination until you can be convinced that the decision is final and are satisfied with the severance arrangements. Often a discharge comes as a surprise. Brace yourself. This is not the time to get emotional. As never before, you need to bargain for your future career. Be prepared to ask your boss some important questions.

Why am I being fired? There are as many reasons for terminating an employee as there are jobs. Possibly the firm is in trouble so that substantial cutbacks have to be made in the workforce. You should at least find out why you are on the hit list. Maybe you have low seniority. On the other hand, your boss may be dissatisfied with your performance. Find out exactly why the employer has decided to terminate you. You ought to have the right to know. Sometimes you can persuade the firm to keep you on. If not, knowing why you were let go will help you decide what to do next.

Can anything be done to save my job? Sometimes a change in your job description or a transfer to another position can be arranged. Has the employer considered the alternatives? The firm already has an investment in a worker: The costs of training a new employee to do the job are not inconsiderable. If you are regarded as a loyal employee, you may get consideration for some other position which you may be qualified to fill. Perhaps a job will open up when business improves.

Can I appeal the decision? Unless you are a member of a union or employed by a government organization, you can probably be dropped for any reason as long as it does not violate some law against discrimination. Only recently have some courts afforded legal protection against unjust dismissal or protected employees against being terminated without just cause. But if your case seems unfair, you should discuss your rights with a competent attorney. If discrimination may be involved, you should talk with an appropriate government agency.

Many companies have procedures under which a termination decision must be reviewed by higher levels, sometimes all the way to the chief executive's office under an "open-door" policy. A few concerns offer impartial arbitration. You should find out whether you have a right to appeal. If the reason for your termination cannot be justified, you may be able to reverse the decision. Find out from the personnel director what can be done to have the matter reconsidered.

What are my termination benefits? Frequently, severance arrangements are negotiable. For example, an executive may be able to stay on the payroll for several months, with the use of a telephone or even a part-time secretary. That can be particularly helpful when you are looking for a new position. Accrued vacation, sick leave or company severance payments are very important to a person being terminated. Sometimes these payments can be augmented by effective bargaining. Even when they are specified in the company's benefit package, an employer may be willing to "buy out" a questionable case. It is certainly worth a try; the employer may decide to avoid an argument about his right to discharge you.

Will my boss give me a good reference? When you are interviewed by prospective employers, they will want to contact your former employer. It is important that you try to get an agreement about who will respond to such enquiries and what will be said. A good reference is crucial. Try to steer such enquiries to someone who will give you a positive recommendation, a person who is familiar with your work and can be trusted to praise you. Since you can never be certain who will be contacted, you should stay on good terms with all of your former associates. They are more than likely to be asked about you.

What can I tell my family? For many people, an immediate problem is how to explain the termination to their friends and family, as well as rationalizing it to themselves. The employer should try to protect the individual's pride. Being let go is destructive enough without being unnecessarily savaged by a punitive boss. Ask your boss for a positive way to explain the facts. This doesn't mean you shouldn't be honest with your family. Tell them why you lost your job and explain what you will be doing to find another. You should be candid with them about your problems so that they can cope with the situation as it affects each of them.

Once you know you are about to be discharged, you will immediately want to concentrate on getting your next job. Send your resumes. Talk to your friends and business contacts. Remember that you are marketing a pretty good product: yourself. Go at it in a businesslike way, packaging all of your credentials and selling your abilities in the job market. With a positive attitude, you are likely to be successful.

At the same time, you might want to ask yourself what you can learn from being fired. It is possible to profit from our failures. Take advantage of the termination experience by reassessing your career strategies. Why were you terminated? What can you discover about your attitude toward work, that particular job, about taking orders? You may decide to change direction, seeking employment in a different field. Perhaps change must take place within yourself. Do you need more education? Being dismissed at least gives you an opportunity to reorient yourself with the working world. In our free society, the responsibility is largely yours.

Mr. Coulson, president of the American Arbitration Association, is author of "The Termination Handbook" (Free Press).

197

6

Protecting Your Company

When Disaster Strikes

By C. R. Reagan

Just as no individual expects to have an accident, no company or plant expects to have a fire, explosion, toxic tank car derailment, tornado damage or other disaster. Yet TV, radio and newspapers remind us that such unhappy events do occur all too frequently. When they do, one immediate and important factor attendant to them is handling the barrage of media personnel who cover such "high news" events. They arrive at the scene with amazing rapidity, all scrambling to be first on the air or in print with statements, interviews, pictures and bulletins describing the facts—and their interpretations of them. I recall the summer evening several years ago when TV and radio personnel came dashing to the chemical plant where I worked for 25 years to cover the crash of a private plane on the plant's property.

This type of disaster scenario can be bewildering to people unaccustomed to dealing with the press. If poorly handled, such events create unfavorable impressions in the public mind that can undo a positive public-relations image that may have been built up painstakingly through many years of community service.

So, what should a company do to be better prepared to cope with an emergency that hopefully will never happen? Advance planning should certainly include, but not be limited to, the following things:

1) Have a list of emergency numbers (fire, police and medical) on hand at the company switchboard. Establish a good relationship with key personnel from these services. If appropriate, give them a tour of your facilities so they understand the layout and any special problems that might relate to traffic control, types of flammable or hazardous materials you use, the fire and medical equipment you have and the types of training your personnel have received.

2) Specify who will be the spokesman for your company. Instruct this person how to deal with the press, how to be interviewed by TV and radio personnel, etc. Practice with simulated interviews is helpful. This practice should emphasize the fact that he probably will have only 30 to 60 seconds on TV to cover the information you wish to communicate. Practice the techniques of how to control an interview rather than be controlled by it.

3) Maintain a current list of the news directors of local TV and radio stations and the business writers and editors of community newspapers. Get acquainted with them, since they are likely to show up at your plant when an emergency strikes. Provide them, during your normal contacts, with a fact sheet about your plant and a description of what you do, as well as telling them whom to contact for plant information.

4) Designate a place where media personnel will be escorted when they arrive at the plant. This location should provide:

    a. Access to telephones (list which ones).

    b. A designated work area.

    c. Access to rest rooms, coffee and refreshments.

    d. Electrical outlets and a desirable section for filming TV interviews.

5) Management's first concern must be the safety of employees, the public and the press. Controls must be exercised to ensure this. This point must be stressed when denying the press access to any areas where hazards exist or emergency activities are in progress.

6) Let the media know when they can expect a news statement or release. Releases should be issued as quickly as pertinent facts can be obtained.

7) The plant disaster plan should identify who will perform specific functions. Some examples are:

a. Determining the need for off-plant emergency personnel (fire, police, medical, etc.).

b. Supervising disaster control and relief activities in various plant areas.

c. Notifying the families of the dead and injured.

d. Setting up and handling the plant communication center.

e. Shutting off electrical systems and pipeline flows, where necessary.

All the above information, and additional items appropriate to your plant or business, should be incorporated into a written disaster plan, with copies given to involved personnel. It is also worthwhile to have annual drills with simulated emergencies to keep everyone aware of their responsibilities, and to give experience to new employees.

Mr. Reagan is a retired Du Pont executive living in Topeka, Kansas.

Corporate Terrorism

By Sam Passow

While business executives often avoid taking preventive steps unless there is a demonstrable threat, there is a growing awareness by corporate executives, especially among the top echelons of the Fortune 500, that there is indeed a need for crisis-management teams to be able to cope with terrorist attacks if and when they happen.

An effective CMT must include executives responsible for finance, risk management, legal matters, personnel, public relations and whoever is earmarked to be the chief negotiator in the event of an extortion threat, be it a bomb or the sabotaging of a product or, perhaps the most difficult challenge, a hostage situation.

According to Richard Clutterbuck, whose book "Kidnap and Ransom: The Response" (Faber & Faber, 1978) is considered by many in the security industry to be the manual on the subject, "with very few exceptions, terrorists view kidnapping as a business transaction where the eventual return of the victim is necessary in order to consummate the deal."

In extortion cases, the fundamental principle is often keeping the threat from the media, which is the terrorist's trump card. A mere rumor, for example, that some foods in a large chain store have been polluted can cause sales losses running into millions of dollars within a week or two.

A company's moral obligation to protect consumers during the crisis might require the recall and/or destruction of the suspect product. Though this cost might seem exorbitant, it is a critical step in regaining public confidence. Johnson & Johnson recalled all its Tylenol capsules, at a cost of $100 million, after cyanide poisoning of some of its capsules left seven Chicago-area residents dead. Although most analysts had predicted Tylenol would never recover from the incident, it now boasts a share of the non-aspirin pain relievers market almost equal to levels recorded before the poisonings. The company's immediate recall and repackaging of the drug was paramount in restoring its market share.

What can a company's CMT do to prepare for corporate terrorism? Peter Goss, who heads the Washington office of Control Risks Ltd., a London-based political-risk analysis firm, contends that a "CMT can best be trained by simulation exercises." One of the best techniques available is a formula developed by the Harvard Law School called the "hypothetical." All those in responsible positions are seated around a horseshoe table facing inward, and are presented with an ongoing hypothetical situation that is developed by a skilled moderator who throws the problems at the executives or officials concerned and carries the story forward in light of their responses.

In a study for Rand Corp., Mr. Clutterbuck notes that "a highly successful 'hypothetical' was run jointly by the British Broadcasting Corp. and the Ford Foundation in late 1979." The seminar took place shortly after the seizure of American hostages at the U.S. Embassy in Tehran, and a seizure of the Iranian Embassy in London was suggested as a hypothetical situation for the workshop participants. No one knew such an incident would actually take place. However, in April 1980, that's exactly what happened.

Participants in this simulation included the senior police officer from Scotland Yard who was destined to handle the actual event when it occurred, army officers, lawyers and journalists—including a BBC television reporter who was at the scene when the rescue attack force went in. Also included was the editor of BBC-TV News, who played a crucial role in working with the attack force. The attack force knew the terrorists were watching television coverage of the event, so the BBC editor agreed to avoid filming scenes of the attack force moving in.

Mr. Goss sees four major areas in which any CMT should be able to operate efficiently:

"The CMT must be able to calculate and prepare a contingency plan to compensate for the loss of management time as senior executives will be taken away from their normal jobs during the crisis.

"There is also the factor of public policy. If a firm gives way and pays a large ransom to keep the matter quiet, the government and other firms may complain that this encourages repetition of the crime.

"Failure to remove the stock or to warn the customers could in the end be even more expensive than paying the extortion demand, as the management would have to justify the morality of its response in the event a customer is poisoned. This, in turn, could lead to heavy legal liabilities if no warning had been given of a known risk.

"Finally, there are the media, which can either be a liability or, if their cooperation is obtained, a powerful asset. In most countries, sadly, the media are under direct government control. In others, they may be totally irresponsible, aiming only to compete for readers and listeners no matter what the risk to human life. It is essential for the public-relations representative of the CMT to know his way around, to know how to best keep unscrupulous or hostile journalists away. If possible, the P.R. rep should develop friendly contacts with some reliable journalists, who can be repaid for their cooperation and forbearance by being the first to get news and exclusive comments. None of this, however, will be achieved unless painstaking preparatory work and development of contacts has been done before there is a crisis."

The first minutes or hours of a crisis are often crucial, and

blundering into negotiations with criminals can be disas-
trous, especially if strategy policy is not set in advance.

---

*Mr. Passow is a free-lance writer in New York who special-
izes in writing about corporate responses to terrorism and
white-collar crime.*

The Hostile Takeover

By James Goldsmith

As enterprises mature, internal bureaucracies often develop. An unfortunate aspect of bureaucracies is that they
tend to become worlds of their own, detached from the realities of the marketplace. Corporate bureaucrats begin to believe that the business that employs them has become an
institution that is their property. Shareholders then become
no more than an inconvenience.

Recently a number of such corporate bureaucracies have
even begun to believe and to state publicly that shareholders lack the wisdom to vote. They have gone so far as
unilaterally to deprive their shareholders, without consulting them, of certain of their basic rights. Several large corporations recently have issued special warrants known as
"poison pills" that deny shareholders the right to consider
tender offers for their shares and that transfer that right to
the board.

Students of history will know of governments that have
believed their voters lacked the wisdom needed to vote, and
therefore have taken over that responsibility on their behalf.

There are always some who believe that hostile corporate
takeovers should be inhibited or forbidden. Should that become the case, management would be entrenched and share-

holders would be deprived of some of their fundamental rights of ownership.

Management is employed by shareholders to manage an enterprise on their behalf. To succeed on a sustained basis, a corporation must market salable products and services, of the right quality and at the right price. Management can achieve this only if, at every level in the corporation, it employs people of the appropriate quality who are satisfied by the working conditions maintained by management. If management fails in these tasks, then the stock market value of the shares of the corporation for which it works will fall. Such a corporation will then be vulnerable to a hostile takeover, and the jobs of the management team will be in jeopardy. If such management is insulated from change, then the corporation will ossify and in due course die.

Of course, everyone, to some degree, fears change. But the ability to face and accommodate change has been one of the pillars on which American prosperity has been built. Many European countries, and others before them, have attempted to restrict freedom and to refuse change. The results are available for evaluation: loss of prosperity and loss of freedom.

The solution to the problems posed by hostile takeovers and the panoply of consequent "shark repellents" is relatively straightforward. First it must be remembered that shareholders are the owners, and that management is employed by them. If management feels that it is in the best interest of shareholders to introduce "shark repellents" into the company's articles of association, then it should explain its reasoning to the owners of the company, namely the shareholders. It is then up to the shareholders to vote on the resolutions.

If, to fight off an unwelcome approach, management wants to buy back blocks of shares at a premium over the market price, then it should explain this to shareholders and submit the proposal to a vote by them. Similarly, if management wishes to embark on what has become known as a policy of "scorched earth" by selling off valuable assets or making defensive acquisitions, then, here again, the proposals should be explained and submitted for a vote by shareholders. It seems wrong that management, to entrench itself, should scorch earth. After all, the earth being scorched belongs not to management, but to shareholders.

If management refuses to explain its case to shareholders and to submit it to a free vote, then the conclusion is obvious: Management is acting for its own survival and is reneging on its contract to protect the interests of those who have entrusted it with that responsibility.

Shareholders would be wise to take steps to eliminate management's conflicts of interest. The most effective way is to align the interests of management with the interests of company owners by creating appropriate stock incentive plans. Management would then be delighted to obtain the best price for its shareholders, as it would also benefit handsomely.

But it should never be forgotten that the best way to avoid a hostile takeover is to manage successfully and, thereby, to earn a sturdy stock market rating.

Sir James is chairman of General Oriental Investments Ltd.

Keeping Down
Legal Costs

By Daniel J. Ryan

The legal establishment and corporate America are sailing on a collision course in which many venerable law firms ultimately will drown in a sea of red ink.

On the one hand, the overhead of law firms has been increasing more rapidly than the inflation rate, resulting in continuously escalating legal fees. Conversely, an expensive corporate litigation explosion has produced an awareness in the business community of the need for more effective legal-cost controls.

This has led to the establishment and expansion of in-house capabilities and reduced business for a considerable number of law firms. But in many instances corporate legal staffs lack both the experience and objectivity to effectively replace outside counsel. This is especially true in the litigation field.

Mutual self-interest dictates that law firms must balance the need for improved productivity from their partners and associates with the client's concern over burgeoning legal expenses. Here are some suggestions for corporate law firms on how to control legal costs and serve clients with fiscal responsibility. Managers should read these suggestions so they know more about their rights as consumers of legal services.

Establish a reasonable number of billable hours the firm expects from its lawyers each year.

Lawyers should not be pressured into billing clients for more than 1,800 hours annually. Law firms that do not establish reasonable standards, but instead promise extra court-approved rewards for herculean hours worked, are likely to bill clients for an inordinate amount of hours, whether or not that amount of time actually was productively expended in the clients' behalf.

Utilize state of the art information-retrieval services to reduce research time and pass on savings to clients.

Many law firms have been slow to incorporate advances in electronic information gathering. Computerized legal research enables firms to obtain research materials expeditiously and economically. Several excellent software programs are commercially available, and law firms not availing themselves of these sophisticated services are making clients bear the cost of archaic, time-consuming research methods. In addition, the use of computers for information management and control of deadlines in litigation, especially in complex cases, is essential to more efficient and less expensive litigation fees.

Make more efficient use of young associates, law clerks, paralegals and law-school students.

Partners, who command high hourly rates, can considerably reduce client fees by delegating research, depositions, trial preparation and other assignments to lower-paid members of the firm, including part-time law-school students. In making these assignments, the senior lawyer in charge of the case should establish time parameters warranted by the importance and complexity of the case.

If the only purpose for the presence of associates, law clerks or paralegals at a trial is to give them exposure to the courtroom proceedings, clients should not be asked to pay for this time. It is improper to have clients, in effect, subsidize a law firm's training program where no tangible benefits accrue to the particular client.

Refer cases outside the law firm's area of expertise to specialized firms that can provide more effective and cost-efficient counsel.

The age of legal specialization—and subspecialization—has arrived. The law firm that is afraid to risk referring a client to a specialized firm because of a particular problem outside the client firm's level of expertise not only does a disservice to the client, but to the advancement of the legal profession as well.

Give clients a cost estimate for each case handled.

Most clients do not want to establish legal precedents, obviously preferring to achieve the most economical legal resolution. For example, few companies would spend $50,000 in legal fees to win a dispute that, if lost, would cost them $5,000. So it is incumbent upon the law firm to make some effort to estimate the cost of litigating each case to its conclusion.

The key element in estimating trial costs is the discovery process, which is laborious and time consuming, but essential for trial preparation. Discovery procedures not only inform the lawyer of the pertinent facts and names of witnesses in the case, but also eliminate the element of surprise by restricting the adversary's ability to present some different version of the facts at the time of trial.

At a minimum, the corporate client should insist that outside counsel outline the discovery program and justify it on a cost-effective basis. Counsel also should advise the client if the discovery process is being abused by the opposition so the client will be able to determine whether the case deserves the kind of time-consuming and expensive response being considered.

Identify at an early stage whether the case should be brought to trial.

This technique involves a certain amount of risk, but can greatly reduce client expenses. Experienced trial counsel can quickly identify, with above average accuracy, those cases that can lead to an equitable settlement instead of a costly trial.

Encourage clients to perform some legal services themselves.

Lawyers often have to dig through voluminous files and spend expensive legal time performing functions that easily could be implemented by corporate employees. For instance, lawyers are often requested to respond to lengthy interrogatories when the client could just as easily prepare the draft of the answers for review by outside counsel.

Law firms serving disenchanted corporate clients have two choices open to them. They can continue bemoaning the current cantankerous state of client relations while charging excessive legal fees to a shrinking corporate base. Or they can get their legal houses in order and generate additional business by serving clients more efficiently than the in-house corporate legal departments they so unwisely excoriate.

Mr. Ryan is managing partner of LaBrum & Doak, a Philadelphia-based law firm specializing in litigation and general civil practice.

Five of the Worst Agreements You Can Make With a Union

By Charles S. Loughran

Through the process of concessionary bargaining, many employers have been able to rid themselves of numerous costly and counterproductive labor contract terms. However, some of the most troublesome and expensive labor contract provisions have been overlooked or given inadequate priority. A selective list inevitably omits some important items, but the following five categories of contract provisions should be at the top of any unionized employer's "hit list" or, if they are not already in its labor contract, the employer's avoidance list:

Joint Union-Management Pension and Health Plans. Joint trusteeship of pension, health-care and other benefit plans was approved by Congress with the passage of the Taft-Hartley Act in 1947. Typically, these are multiemployer plans involving a number of employers in one industry funded by specific hourly, weekly or monthly employer contributions. These plans are commonly considered by employees (and even some contributing employers) to be "union plans." Although the employer contributes substantial sums to the plans, the union rather than the employer is generally given credit by employees for being their benefactor in these key benefit areas.

A serious disadvantage of these partnerships is loss of

employer flexibility in administering the health plans. For example, an employer cannot pursue alternative pension-funding strategies or health-care self-insurance arrangements without the concurrence of union and other management trustees.

This defect pales, however, in comparison with the financial risks imposed by the 1980 Multi-Employer Pension Plan Amendments to the Employee Retirement Income Security Act. These amendments place financial "withdrawal liability" on employers who leave a joint union-management pension plan that is underfunded. Because a great number of union-management plans are seriously underfunded, any employer would be foolhardy to sign on to an underfunded plan at this late date. Employers already contributing to underfunded plans may find the current price of withdrawal to be small in comparison with possible future liability.

Automatic Cost Escalating Provisions. Labor contract wage and benefit indexing has become common in labor contracts. The most prevalent and expensive of these is the cost of living wage adjustment or "COLA." There are other escalators, however, which are not quite so obvious. Shift differentials, meal allowances and other special payments, which are keyed to wage levels, automatically escalate with negotiated increases. As wage increases are negotiated, the "rollup" effect on these benefits is seldom recognized by either union representatives or employees as constituting any real improvement in compensation, yet their costs are substantial.

The major drawback of automatic cost escalators, especially COLAs, is that the employer's labor costs can, and do, increase at times when the employer's profits and ability to pay are stagnant or even decreasing. The history of auto, steel and other manufacturing industries in the highly inflationary years of the late '70s and early '80s is evidence of the havoc such escalators can reap.

More Pay for Unworked Time. High hourly wages paid by employers in many industries would often be tolerable if they constituted the total payment for labor. However, the cost of indirect wages and non-wage benefits has grown to astounding proportions. For example, going into its 1984 negotiations with the United Auto Workers, General Motors Corp.'s average straight-time hourly wage rate was slightly less than $13 an hour. GM's average hourly labor cost, including all wage and benefit payments, amounted to nearly $23 an hour. The payroll "burden" was thus an astronomical 77%. While higher than average, that percentage figure is not terribly out of line with other unionized employers.

A significant portion of the payroll burden is contributed by pay for unworked time. Included in this are pay for vacations, holidays, sick leave, union business, wash-up and other personal time, as well as premiums for a variety of reasons such as "call-outs" and inconvenient schedules.

Work Jurisdictional Limitations. When employers talk about "costly work practices," they invariably point to agreements, understandings or traditions that limit in some way the type and scope of work employees can perform. Classic examples are restrictions on maintenance and construction craftsmen in performing work outside their respective trades. Other examples include departmental jurisdictional barriers and job descriptions that restrict employees in one department or classification from performing work outside their respective areas. These restrictions invariably result in the underutilization of employees and the need to hire more personnel.

Union Representation on Corporate Boards. The election of union leaders as corporate directors is a recent and relatively infrequent phenomenon. Nevertheless, sufficient precedents have been established to suggest that this foolish practice may proliferate. The leading example is, of course, the Chrysler Corp.-UAW agreement. With its corporate back to the wall in 1979, Chrysler agreed to place Douglas Fraser, then UAW president, on its board. When Mr. Fraser retired, the new UAW president, Owen Bieber, was soon elected to fill what must now be regarded (at least by the union) as "labor's seat" on the Chrysler board.

Regardless of Chrysler's trust in the discretion of Messrs.

Fraser and Bieber, no employer can reasonably expect a union leader to refrain from using confidential and sensitive information for labor's own purposes. Union-management cooperation is a worthy goal, but not in the board room.

Justice Felix Frankfurter once said, "Wisdom too often never comes and therefore one ought not to reject it merely because it comes late." The wisdom in recognizing improvident labor agreements and the determination to correct them can never come too late.

Mr. Loughran is director of corporate industrial relations for Louisiana-Pacific Corp. and is author of "Negotiating a Labor Contract: A Management Handbook" (BNA Books, 1984).

7

Family and Friends

Sex and Romance in the Office and Plant

By Mortimer R. Feinberg and
Aaron Levenstein

Management has never been quite sure how to handle sex and romance. But then who is?

Now, however, business is in a bind. Contemporary culture presses management not to intrude on employees' private lives. At the same time, without experiencing the pleasures or the guilt, management may be legally liable for "sexual harassment."

No self-respecting employer would approve of harassment in any form, much less in sexual behavior. Unfortunately, the line between harassment and voluntary involvement is not always easily discerned. Must a company now scrutinize attachments among its employees to distinguish between the "harasser" and the smitten romantic pleading his or her cause?

The influx of women into management ranks has multiplied contacts between the sexes. The greater overtness about homosexuality in our society also increases the potential for harassment or voluntary sexual involvement. Under existing law, according to Robert H. Faley of Purdue University, sexual demands made by a supervisor on an employee of the opposite sex are discriminatory, but "where a supervisor who is bisexual places these conditions on both genders...the insistence on sexual favors would not constitute sex discrimination."

Advocates of traditional morality simply condemn all sexual-physical involvements among people on the work force. In conducting a mini-survey among executives, we encountered only a few respondents who took that position. One said:

"I don't believe in forcing my beliefs on others, but I do acknowledge the responsibility to cultivate a sound moral base within a profitable company. I think a strong moral code is good business—it fosters security and fairness, and provides a stronger base for setting expectations than merely profit considerations."

But most of our respondents feel otherwise; their primary concern is the impact on work performance and company reputation. A recently retired executive of an international electrical appliance firm writes: "Once, when I was general manager, I had as a manager of manufacturing a fast-moving, aggressive and handsome man. He was courteous as well as demanding. He was well liked by the work force.

"One night I received a phone call from his wife telling me that her husband was running around with a secretary in the plant, and she wanted me to fire the secretary. In fact, she said, the same thing had happened in another plant, in another city, and she had asked the general manager to fire the girl, which he did.

"I told her that if I fired anybody it would be her husband. She never called again."

He explains his reasons. He had, of course, heard rumors of the affair, but it was having absolutely no effect on company operations. The secretary was competent, and so was the man. "The wife was in truth a bitch," he writes, "and we knew for a fact that she was treating her husband badly. Inasmuch as the work performance of both individuals was not being adversely affected, I did not feel it necessary to do anything. I never had the slightest intention to fire either."

But is the company really untouched by the affair? When an executive fixes his roving eye on the secretary of a colleague, the first to be upset is likely to be his own secretary. One executive who became involved with a secretary confesses that his relationship with her boss was impaired. The colleague was afraid his confidences would be breached to her lover.

On the other hand, some rather straight-laced executives have been frank to acknowledge that on learning of a peer's affair with an attractive employee, resentment has stirred: "Why with him (or her), and not me?"

Of 112 respondents to our questions, 57 said yes when asked, "Do you believe in a policy of absolute hands-off in cases of simple romance?" Thirty-nine said no, and 16 avoided any answer. But the same alternatives with reference to "more complex relationships" brought a response of only 32 saying hands-off and 62 saying intervene, with 19 remaining silent.

Recognizing that "something is going on" is apparently not very difficult in the tight little society of a business firm. As the vice president of a communications network said to us, the signs are there to be read: Suddenly a woman who is not in the formal chain of command begins to show up at meetings alongside an executive. Or someone in a distant department is now making frequent appearances to deliver memos. He and she are staying after hours. Discerning observers notice that two pairs of eyes are meeting more often, followed by cryptic Mona Lisa smiles. Or the executive, who once boasted that his door is always open, now spends more time behind a closed door, and not alone. Any of these is enough to start the millwheels of rumor turning.

On the basis of the anecdotal material submitted to us, there are four gradations of involvement:

1) Sexual harassment—unwanted or uninvited sexual attentions, behavior that is illegal and impermissible. If it takes place, the company can protect itself only by having previously promulgated a policy of disapproval and by taking prompt remedial action, possible discharge of the culprit after warnings to desist.

2) Legitimate courtship, aimed at marriage, by two single individuals. Companies often take pride in the number of marriages among their personnel. This relationship becomes problematic only if the romance ends unhappily, creating an atmosphere of stress not only for the couple but for

their co-workers. Some companies still have a policy that, with marriage, one of the spouses must leave, but this is being challenged by feminists and may, under some circumstances, be illegal as discriminatory since usually it is the woman who goes. One bank president told us that his policy is not to hire spouses, but no one is let go for marrying a fellow employee.

3) A sexual relationship without benefit of clergy by two unmarried people. In most such cases, the relationship is carried on in clandestine meetings off the premises; in a growing number of cases, but still relatively few, the parties live together openly in the same quarters.

4) The illicit affair, involving at least one married person. Some executives are concerned largely about the psychological disruption a broken marriage may produce, possibly leading in turn to work impairment.

It is primarily the last two categories that are viewed with apprehension by most managements. Of our 112 respondents, 76 replied that people in their organizations had been admonished by their superiors to "observe caution"; 50 stated that warnings were issued to discontinue the relationship. A dozen reported that the relationship was penalized by a denial of promotion; 20 indicated that other action, including discharge, had been taken.

Asked whether their companies had experienced adverse effects because of such relationships, a surprisingly large number—almost a third—gave no reply. But 32 did say that sexual involvements had led to charges of favoritism, while 52 reported no such experience. A majority of those answering felt that "scandal mongering" had indeed resulted—44 yes to 41 no. A vote of 45 to 43 said morale had been undermined.

There seems to be overwhelming agreement that rank in the hierarchy is of considerable importance, for example, in producing charges of favoritism. There is virtually no problem when the parties are among the rank and file. But if they are in management, particularly where the relationship is between superior and subordinate, there is much concern. Higher authority often seeks a way out by transferring the subordinate to another unit or branch, if the company is large enough.

Many companies will tolerate a relationship between superior and subordinate if it is not conducted on company premises; does not utilize company facilities, such as a company-rented apartment; involves no company funds, for example, use of business credit cards or expense accounts to entertain a sex partner; does not divert energy from effective work performance; is not furthered on company time; does not damage the company's public image; is not deliberately flaunted in a way that offends the sensibilities of others in the organization.

This approach, of course, is based on the theory that what individuals do off the premises and on their own time is no concern of the employer. It recalls the story told of George Horace Lorimer, editor of the Saturday Evening Post. One installment of a serialized novel had ended with an account of a beautiful secretary having dinner with her boss; the next installment began with their having breakfast together. Readers raised a hue and cry that the magazine, a pillar of respectability, had abandoned its moral values. Mr. Lorimer answered in an editorial statement: "The Saturday Evening Post is not responsible for what its characters do between installments."

Most top managements prefer to handle discipline for sexual conduct (or misconduct, as some prefer to call it) with little fanfare. Overwhelmingly, our respondents say that their admonitions and discussions usually lead to resignation rather than discharge. The top executives are usually the last to know about the offensive behavior. Therefore it is not necessary to strip the individual of his epaulets publicly; the spectators will have no difficulty deducing from the resignation what happened behind the scenes.

Mr. Feinberg is chairman of BFS Psychological Associates, a New York consulting firm. Mr. Levenstein is professor emeritus of management at Baruch College.

The Perils and Rewards of Executive Friendships

By Mortimer R. Feinberg
and Aaron Levenstein

The president of a savings and loan company calls friendship with subordinates "a high-risk, low-reward situation" that jeopardizes both parties. "How," he asks, "would the subordinate be perceived by his peers if he has a close relationship with the boss?"

The head of a leading food distribution company says: "I never made friends in the Army as a captain and I don't in my company. If you get too close, it is difficult to separate yourself when they get killed or, in the company, when you may have to fire a friend. However, don't quote me by name because I don't want people to think I'm an aloof S.O.B."

Executives, like all humans, need friends. They need confidants with whom they can let down their hair, reveal personal uncertainties that periodically assail even the most stalwart spirits and seek advice and encouragement.

Yet friendship between superiors and subordinates is problematic. Emerson's epigram, "to have a friend, you must be a friend," neatly underscores the reciprocity involved in the relationship. Friends do not mete out "rewards" to each other on the basis of "to each according to his just deserts." But executives must.

Inevitably the time comes when the executive must say no in circumstances where the friend would say yes. For executives, saying yes too often is a costly business. No matter how deeply personal the relationship between superior and subordinate, the moment of truth may eventually call for the turndown, the refusal to grant a pay increase or a promotion, the criticism of work poorly done, the decision, perhaps, to terminate.

Friendship has difficulty surviving in the competitive atmosphere that often colors internal company relationships. A former vice president of a textile manufacturing firm says: "In a competitive situation, with people competing for the narrow, limited number of positions at the top, it's best to separate yourself from too much personal contact. This doesn't mean that you should be aloof; rather be open, talk about business subjects but keep your fears and personal problems to yourself."

To reveal them may make you vulnerable to someone who may be your rival tomorrow. At the very least, executives fear that by such a display, even to a friend, they may undermine the image of strong leadership their subordinate needs and wants. Far safer to remain silent about the trouble with the wife or the arrest of a son in a marijuana bust.

Moreover, some who are considered friends often turn out to be sycophants who want to be close to the seat of power. Retired executives often find that their erstwhile golf partners suddenly start playing tennis on Sundays. The suspicion that would-be friends are merely self-seekers leads some executives to avoid all friendships and to settle for socializing.

Other executives, however, reject emotional celibacy and view friendship itself as one of the rewards of an active business life.

The president of a large communications enterprise thinks he has found the way to accommodate his personal need for friendship with his organization's need for tough-minded control. "I can drink with a man at night and still criticize him in the morning," he says. But apparently this is possible only because he is highly selective. "I have never had a friend whose professional competence I could not respect. Once that element is present, I can level with him on his performance."

In fact, some executives find it easier to hold a criticism session with a friend. They believe that criticizing constructively is itself an act of friendship that serves both the friend and the organization.

"The hardest task I ever faced," says the CEO of a major aerospace firm, "was to deal with a close friend who worked for us and who became an alcoholic. After we paid all the bills for his unsuccessful hospitalization to 'dry out,' I had to let him go. But sometime later, he came by to thank me for forcing him to get his act together. We are still close friends."

Newly-promoted executives often face the issue of retaining friendships with people who were formerly peers. Those who refuse to end the relationship note that they cannot continue "friendship as usual." Out of their experience, these guidelines emerge:

1) Sooner or later, preferably sooner, sit down and have a frank discussion of the new circumstances. If necessary, certain topics may have to be viewed henceforth as "off limits"—for example, reports on inner-circle conferences, confidential information about other employees, subordinates or peers. Where confidences are still exchanged, their "classified" nature must be strictly observed.

2) Discuss the areas in which friendship is not to be invoked—for example, evaluations of performance, the making of assignments, opportunities for training and development. Neither individual can benefit ultimately if others can conclude correctly that favoritism is occurring; both will lose the respect they need if they are to do their jobs.

3) Both individuals must be prepared to pay a price for the friendship. There may be snide remarks, but if the friendship is valued, that is a small enough price. When the comments are unfair, the friendship can continue undisturbed.

4) But if a friend compromises his superior, it should be clearly understood in advance that the consequences may be more severe than usual. When one of President Johnson's aides became involved in a homosexual scandal, he was

promptly banished from the White House. After Mr. Johnson left office, the friendship was resumed.

5) Above all, true friends recognize that they must protect each other and forestall undeserved criticism. President Truman lost much ground because of what came to be called "cronyism." The special relationship of friendship on the job must be circumspect—conducted with a due respect for the feelings of others.

Such policies reflect an important fact about the nature of friendship itself. The relationship is its own reward; its purpose is not utilitarian. The issue among friends is not how they can use each other but how they can serve each other. Nothing in this concept need contravene the purpose or the effectiveness of a business relationship involving friends.

Aristotle said that friendship is "indispensable to life." The executive who attempts to dispense with it in business, the activity that consumes most of his waking hours, would be seriously impoverished.

Mr. Feinberg is chairman of BFS Psychological Associates, a New York consulting firm. Mr. Levenstein is professor emeritus of management at Baruch College.

Kids plus Careers Needn't Keep Mom in Arrears

By Claudia P. Feurey

An article in The Wall Street Journal once described a working mother—a major account executive for an advertising firm—who almost missed an important meeting because she had to dash out into the snow to buy diapers for her child. Her housekeeper called and said they had run out. The mother left the office, spent $20 on cab fare for a $10 box of diapers and arrived back at the office feeling as if she'd "been to California and back."

The tone of the article was summed up by an "expert" who was quoted as saying that most women find combining career and family an impossible situation. "I'm not sure," said the expert, "how any woman can avoid being overwhelmed. Simply dropping out may be the only alternative."

Maybe. But there are many women with children doing well out there in law firms, accounting offices, government and other professional capacities. Of course it is difficult for a professional woman to manage a successful career and be a mother. But women in management have an edge they might not be using to the full advantage: They can put their management skills to use in managing their lives as working mothers.

Taking a managerial approach to home life doesn't mean you have to haul in McKinsey & Co. to do a work-flow study on your kids. And it certainly isn't recommending a tough-cookie approach to home and hearth. Far from being callous, an effective management approach to child rearing is the most loving, caring and respectful course a professional woman can take. When arrangements are slapdash, when no one knows what to do next, when Mommy is too torn and crazed to be effective either as an investment banker or as a mother, then everyone suffers.

If the woman who almost missed her meeting had paid more attention to managing her inventory (diapers) and to hiring an employee who could take expected initiative (going out and buying the diapers), she probably would not have ended up in such a frazzled state.

A three-step management approach is required for the effective manager-mother:

1) *A feasibility study.* Some jobs in some companies may not be compatible with family life. Sixty-hour weeks, a two-hour commute and a heavy travel schedule don't leave much time for kids. (Of course, this is true for men as well as women.)

Does the culture of your organization support families? Management attitude can make or break a company as a place where women can have both families and careers. While management should not be expected to go out of its way to accommodate unreasonable demands, it is generally in a company's interest to ease the transition when its employees become parents.

2) *Making your decision and setting your priorities.* If you decide you can work, do you still want to? They may not get into this at Wharton, but if you have other sources of income, you do not have to work at a particular job. There is no disgrace in not working or in working part time and devoting the rest of your time to your family and home.

If you decide to work, however, get your priorities straight. As a managerial mother, you may not be able to keep up your previous social life, be den mother to the Cub Scouts or see every play that comes to town. If family and career come first, carefully evaluate the costs and benefits of other claims on your time.

3) *Implementation.* The next step is organizing your life so that you can combine home, children and career with the minimum strain.

Decide what your child-care needs are. If your job involves late nights, early meetings or extensive travel, then be sure your husband or your help can cover for you during these times. Or make standing arrangements with other reliable sources.

Bite the bullet and pay for the best child care you can afford. It is astonishing how many high-income families try to make do with ad hoc arrangements or bottom-of-the-barrel help. Would you trust the person you hire to deal with an emergency or get a sick child to the doctor? If not, you have made a mistake. Hire the best person you can afford, treat her well and let her do her job.

Have a reliable temporary agency or nurses' registry on call for those days the nanny is ill. These agencies exist in virtually every community and may be a lot less hassle than getting your mother to come over on a snowy Tuesday.

Ferret out every neighborhood store that delivers and set up local charge accounts at these stores.

Learn to appreciate the virtues of takeout food.

Even with the most sophisticated management approach, there will be times when your husband is out of town, when your three-year-old has thrown up on your best suit and you are late for work. It is easy to succumb to playing the part of the working heroine, a martyr for the movement. When this happens, it is wise to think of the many, many women who are working—and often raising their kids alone—without the privileges and the psychic and financial rewards of management positions. At these times, look at your family, look at your accomplishments and count your blessings.

Being a working mother will never be a simple task. It may not be fair that the lion's share of child rearing falls on the mother, but it happens. And if it happens to you, don't check your management skills at your own front door.

Mrs. Feurey is vice president and director of information for the New York office of the Committee for Economic Development.

How Businesswomen Can Husband Their Energies

By Marilyn Machlowitz

Corporate wives traditionally have provided their business-man husbands with all kinds of emotional and practical support. The men may make specific requests: "Hey, hon, can you bring my dinner jacket to the office?" They may also be the beneficiaries of assistance they may not even be aware of: their wives' taking the kids to Grandma's when peace and quiet would be helpful at home.

When women assume demanding careers, they, too, stand to gain from having supportive corporate spouses. They, too, can use helpers with the logistics of life who shuffle the day's appointments to catch the school play and provide caring attention that can be counted on.

Corporate husbands actually have an edge on nonworking wives in providing some types of support. Since most corporate husbands work, they tend to "speak the same language" as their wives and understand the "turf" the women walk on. A corporate husband can expand his wife's range of contacts by drawing upon his own business acquaintances.

When it comes to serving as a sounding board, both his ability to decipher male codes and his business experience may prove beneficial to his wife. In so serving, it is more important for him to listen than to respond. Instant answers—e.g., "Why don't you just quit?"—are less satisfying than one might think. They can strike a woman as a device to curtail discussion, rather than as a useful suggestion. Nor is advice necessarily needed—or desired.

A man must determine which role he might best fulfill on any given occasion: lightning rod (to absorb the anger she cannot afford to vent at work), devil's advocate, career coach or sympathetic consoler. It can be hard to read a spouse's mind, so sometimes it will be necessary to ask outright.

A corporate husband might understand, too, that after a day of dealing with colleagues and subordinates, his wife may simply be "peopled-out," just as he may be. She may need some time to unwind before recounting the details of the day or planning the evening ahead. An imbalance can occur when one partner returns home refreshed and raring to go and the other races home without the transitional activity of a drink at the club, a squash match or even a tranquil commute. Corporate couples usually accept the reality that either or both parties may be emotionally unavailable from time to time.

A husband's knowledge, too, of what hectic, harried business travel can be like averts the envy home-based wives sometimes experience and express. A homemaker might wonder, "Why is it that he gets to go to New Delhi and I only get to go to New Jersey?" Anyone who has traveled on business extensively knows that a meeting in New Delhi and an awful lot of other places, often as not, might as well be in New Jersey.

Corporate husbands can also do much of what their wives have always done. They can juggle their schedules, for instance, to provide coverage at home. One woman who travels a lot was concerned that back-to-back trips would leave a 12-year-old daughter without a parent around for two weeks. Happily, the woman's husband had the flexibility, personally and professionally, to rearrange his plans.

Men may also be asked to accompany their wives on trips to meetings or to client dinners in town. Many men report being glad to dine at fine restaurants, regardless of the reason. Once there, however, they must make sure they leave the spotlight to their wives. Playing second fiddle can be extremely uncomfortable for someone unaccustomed to the role. Conversely, if he enjoys enough recognition on his own turf, not getting any on hers may be something of a relief.

It makes sense to determine which events are mandatory and which ones can be skipped. One physician accompanied his wife to the annual dinner of her professional association. He grumbled about having to make a "command performance." Since the gathering was huge—and his wife table-hopped anyway—his presence may not have been necessary.

Corporate husbands can also make sure that their working wives aren't doing double duty. It is very common for women who are former homemakers to tack on a full-time job without letting up on domestic duties. It would be hard to describe a surer prescription for overload and overwork than imposing an additional role on top of the traditional role.

Husbands might suggest hiring household help or, if such help already is available, increasing the service by several days a week. Corporate husbands can state explicitly that a lower standard of household cleanliness fails to faze them. One couple admits that their only goal is to stay "one step ahead of the sanitation inspector."

Men can, of course, also increase their own level of participation in domestic chores.

What most women emphasize is that it is essential for their spouses to assume some of the mental work of maintaining a household, and not just the menial work. The issue may not be who stops at the gourmet takeout shop on the way home from work, but who remembers that it has to be done, designates what is to be bought and delegates the task.

Working wives may hinder their husbands' desires to do their part. Some women have trouble letting go of what may have been within their purview, such as cozy chats with the children. Many other women make the mistake of assuming that their husbands don't want to lighten their loads. Once working women accept their husbands' abilities—and agility—in these areas, the old joke that every woman needs a wife may fail to seem funny.

Ms. Machlowitz, who counsels, consults and writes on career-related issues from New York, frequently conducts programs for executives and their spouses at conferences and conventions.

The Busy Executive as Husband and Father

By Mortimer R. Feinberg and
Aaron Levenstein

Recently the vice president for marketing at an international company was virtually ordered to cancel a long-delayed trip to Bermuda with his wife. On the eve of his departure his president told him that the chairman of the board, based in Europe, would be flying in on the Concorde at 10 a.m. the next day and would be leaving at 4 p.m. the same day. "He wants to hear us make the presentation of the new marketing program," said the president, "and only you can do it." The vice president demurred, arguing that his assistant could do the job just as well. "Do you want a career or a file cabinet?" asked the president. Undaunted by the suggestion that he might wind up as a clerk, the man left for Bermuda. On his return, he learned that his assistant now had caught the admired attention of the chairman.

We all know such stories, and of the tensions between business obligation and family commitment. The Wall Street Journal and the Gallup Organization have reported that a substantial majority of executives surveyed believe success in business requires the making of "personal and family sacrifices." The data suggests that "chief executives typically work 60 to 70 hours a week, travel six to 10 days a month and give up many of their weekends."

This is not just a product of the American culture but is

characteristic of all industrial societies. It is a culmination of the process that began when the Industrial Revolution took the father out of the home and left the mother to raise, cosset and discipline the children. Now many women, too, are pursuing demanding careers. So both men and women are having to make family sacrifices if they wish to succeed in many organizations.

Yet many executives do find a way, despite some ragged edges, to fit a satisfying family life into the pattern of a successful career. They do it by recognizing that life does not always require the big, dramatic solution to problems, that outcomes often depend on doing a series of small things consistently. Here are some of the practices that have become almost habitual with them:

1) They do not hide behind alibis. They are frank with members of the family and discuss conflicts between home and job whenever they arise.

2) They schedule some time exclusively for the family. These may be short intervals or sustained periods like long weekends and vacations. On such occasions, they do not allow work to interrupt, except in the most extreme emergencies.

3) Even when working at home, they take breaks to renew contact. They recall Eleanor Roosevelt's advice to a friend in the armed services: "When you go home and get engrossed in work, see that you stop long enough now and then—even when she is working with you—to make her feel she is first in your life, even more important than saving the world. Every woman wants to be first to someone sometime in her life." Mrs. Roosevelt had reason to know.

4) They pay attention to small ceremonial family events. Remembering birthdays, bringing home flowers, making bright conversation at the dinner table, arranging to dine out on an anniversary—such activities are perfectly consistent with the skills that have made the husband a captain of industry.

5) When traveling on business, they call home frequently. And the conversation is more than perfunctory: It deals with substantive family matters; allows the wife to

get things off her chest, if necessary; demonstrates an interest in each of the family members.

6) They share part of their business life with the family. Of course, they do not try to relive the day. But they assume that their wives and children are interested and intelligent, and want a general knowledge of what is happening to the husband or parent.

7) They make significant use of family time. Just as the executive knows the value of his working time, so too he seeks to make the most effective possible use of his time at home. He remains as wide-awake to the interests of spouse and children as he would to those of a customer.

In short, the basic instruments he must use, at home as in the office, are his executive skills. Two are involved: the ability to communicate and the ability to delegate.

The first requires a facility in maintaining contact. What counts, however, is not necessarily frequency of contact but true depth of association when contact is made. The second skill, the art of delegating, begins with the executive's definition of what he may and what he should not delegate.

If an executive decides that family responsibilities are tasks that only he can handle, then the home can take as firm a place in his schedule of activities as any other of his non-delegable activities. And the same principle applies as with all other non-delegable tasks: If a conflict of demands requires that one must be neglected at a given moment, there is a clear understanding that the executive must compensate for the omission at the earliest possible moment.

Much will be gained as top management clarifies its own policy and determines what it expects of its people. It cannot simultaneously demand of its executives the impeccable domestic behavior of a Presbyterian minister and total dedication to the needs of the company. The criteria should be made clear in advance to those who seek promotion and to those already in the executive suite.

But the primary responsibility continues to rest on the individual to define his own values. Besieged by a press and media that denigrate his business efforts and that extol the virtues of personalism, a butt of soap operas and women's magazines, the executive must make his choice. Specifically, he must answer these questions:

Is he prepared to live with the tension that will come if he strives to be both top man in his organization and the beloved patriarch of his home?

Given the new pressures that exist in the business scene of the 1980s, is he prepared to withstand the demands and reproaches of peers, subordinates and superiors if he opts for family priorities?

If he decides to take vows as a "monk of industry," will he be able to live with the judgment that his family and the community may render, and can he gain his satisfactions from knowing that his business activity, as a whole, serves his nation and ultimately his family?

As Americans wrestle with this kind of problem, it may be useful to remember that a society needs all kinds of people—the footloose and the home-bound.

Mr. Feinberg, chairman of BFS Psychological Associates, is co-author, with Richard F. Dempewolff, of "Corporate Bigamy" (Morrow). Mr. Levenstein is a professor of management at Baruch College.

References

The following articles have been reprinted by permission of *The Wall Street Journal*, © Dow Jones & Company, Inc.

1

1. "Keep a Watch on Your Most Precious Resource," Andrew S. Grove (September 12, 1983).

2. "Stamina: The Executive's Ultimate Resource," Mortimer R. Feinberg and Aaron Levenstein (February 22, 1982).

3. "Whoever Is Irreplaceable Should Be Replaced," Everett T. Suters (October 10, 1983).

4. "Conversation: The Key to Better Business Writing," John Louis DiGaetani (February 8, 1982).

5. "A Practical Guide to Using Your Time More Efficiently," Robert D. Reid (January 24, 1983).

6. "How Do You Know When to Rely on Your Intuition?" Mortimer R. Feinberg and Aaron Levenstein (June 21, 1982).

7. "How to Make Your Next Speech One to Remember," Ralph Proodian (October 8, 1984).

8. "The Workaholic Boss: An 18-Hour-a-Day Menace," Jack Falvey (May 10, 1982).

9. "A Lifetime of Learning to Manage Effectively," Ralph Z. Sorenson (February 28, 1983).

10. "Confessions of a McKinsey & Co. Consultant,"
    Frank R. Beaudine (October 1, 1984).

11. "Mealing and Dealing: Beware of the Business Lunch,"
    Martin H. Bauman (October 17, 1983).

12. "The Art of Constructive Procrastination,"
    Ross A. Webber (August 23, 1982).

2

1. "Steel Collar Workers: The Lessons From Japan,"
   Kenichi Ohmae (February 16, 1982).

2. "One Company's Quest for Improved Quality,"
   John A. Young (July 25, 1983).

3. "A Revolutionary Way to Streamline the Factory,"
   Richard J. Schonberger (November 15, 1983).

4. "The Big Revolution on the Factory Floor,"
   Thomas M. Hout and George Stalk Jr. (July 12, 1982).

5. "To Exploit New Technology, Know When to Junk the Old,"
   Richard N. Foster (May 2, 1983).

6. "Quality Control Circles: They Work and Don't Work,"
   Kenichi Ohmae (March 29, 1982).

7. "Process Design as Important as Product Design,"
   John Mayo (October 29, 1984).

8. "Don't Expect Too Much From Your Computer System,"
   Richard L. Van Horn (October 25, 1982).

9. "A Slip of the Chip on Computer Spread Sheets Can Cost Millions,"
   Robert M. Freeman (August 20, 1984).

3

1. "To Raise Productivity, Try Saying Thank You,"
   Jack Falvey (December 6, 1982).

2. "People Express Grows Bigger Without Getting Fat,"
   Donald Burr (January 7, 1985).

3. "Sobering Advice on Office Alcoholics,"
   Nicholas A. Pace, M.D. (November 19, 1984).

4. "How to Make Criticism Sessions Productive,"
   J. Stephen Morris (October 12, 1981).

5. "So You're Afraid to Criticize Your Boss,"
   Hendrie Weisinger and Norman M. Lobsenz
   (May 3, 1982).

6. "Keeping Favoritism and Prejudice Out of
   Evaluations,"
   Andrew S. Grove (February 27, 1984).

7. "How to Live With Those Mercurial Mavericks,"
   James E. Seitz (April 4, 1983).

8. "Out of the Water and Into the Office,"
   Peter Baida (October 31, 1983).

9. "Green Over Gray Needn't Lead to a Clash,"
   Marilyn Machlowitz (April 11, 1983).

10. "The Proper Distance Between Boss and Secretary,"
    Mortimer R. Feinberg and Aaron Levenstein
    (September 19, 1983).

11. "How Executives Can Meet With Success,"
    Jack Falvey (July 2, 1984).

12. "Transforming Your Employees Through Dynamic
    Leadership,"
    Mortimer R. Feinberg and Aaron Levenstein
    (November 26, 1984).

4

1. "The Risks and Advantages of Cooperative Ventures," Robert J. Conrads and Amir Mahini (January 16, 1984).

2. "Test Marketing: Your Product May Do Better Without It,"
Solomon Dutka and Richard L. Lysaker
(August 27, 1984).

3. "Corporate Planning Needn't Be an Executive Straitjacket,"
John M. Stengrevics (September 26, 1983).

4. "Transform Leaden Strategies Into Golden Opportunities,"
Kenichi Ohmae (December 24, 1984).

5. "Disorganized Like a Fox: The Sly Boss,"
Jack Falvey (September 17, 1984).

6. "Superstars and Lone Rangers Rescue Dull Enterprises,"
Rosabeth Moss Kanter (January 23, 1984).

7. "Hisao Tsubouchi, Japan's Mr. Turnaround,"
Adam Meyerson (January 10, 1983).

5

1. "What You Can and Can't Learn From Interviews,"
   Martin H. Bauman (August 16, 1982).

2. "What to Do When the Executive Recruiter Calls,"
   Frank R. Beaudine (December 27, 1982).

3. "What to Do When You're Looking for a Job,"
   Robert M. Hochheiser (January 17, 1983).

4. "The Agonizing Decision of Cutting Corporate Staff,"
   Carol Hymowitz (July 26, 1982).

5. "Hiring a Teen-ager for the Summer,"
   Frank J. Macchiarola (June 13, 1983).

6. "Bringing Retired Talent Back to the Fore,"
   Phillip Shatz (December 5, 1983).

7. "There's No Room for Loyalty in Business,"
   Harvey Gittler (January 28, 1985).

8. "If Right to Fire Is Abused, Uncle Sam May Step In,"
   Thomas R. Horton (June 11, 1984).

9. "Hitting Rock Bottom After Making It to the Top,"
   James F. Turner (August 6, 1984).

10. "Questions You Hope You Never Have to Ask,"
    Robert Coulson (January 25, 1982).

6

1. "When Disaster Strikes, Be Prepared,"
   C. R. Reagan (January 9, 1984).

2. "Corporate Terrorism: Thinking About the
   Unthinkable,"
   Sam Passow (March 26, 1984).

3. "Hostile Takeovers: Easier to Swallow Than Poison
   Pills,"
   James Goldsmith (February 11, 1985).

4. "An Insider's Guide to Legal Service Savings,"
   Daniel J. Ryan (August 13, 1984).

5. "Five of the Worst Agreements You Can Make With a
   Union,"
   Charles S. Loughran (December 10, 1984).

7

1. "Sex and Romance in the Office and Plant,"
   Mortimer R. Feinberg and Aaron Levenstein
   (November 29, 1982).

2. "The Perils and Rewards of Executive Friendships,"
   Mortimer R. Feinberg and Aaron Levenstein
   (August 9, 1982).

3. "Kids Plus Careers Needn't Keep Mom in Arrears,"
   Claudia P. Feurey (June 4, 1984).

4. "How Businesswomen Can Husband Their Energies,"
   Marilyn Machlowitz (August 22, 1983).

5. "How Busy Executives Can Manage on the Home
   Front,"
   Mortimer R. Feinberg and Aaron Levenstein
   (June 15, 1981).